THE ELEMENTS OF USER EXPERIENCE

SECOND EDITION

USER-CENTERED DESIGN
FOR THE WEB AND BEYOND

Written and Illustrated by
Jesse James Garrett

The Elements of User Experience: User-Centered Design for the Web and Beyond, Second Edition

Jesse James Garrett

New Riders 1249 Eighth Street
Berkeley, CA 94710
510/524-2178
510/524-2221 (fax)

Find us on the Web at: www.newriders.com
To report errors, please send a note to errata@peachpit.com
New Riders is an imprint of Peachpit, a division of Pearson Education.

Project Editor: Michael J. Nolan
Development Editor: Rose Weisburd
Production Editor: Tracey Croom
Copyeditor: Doug Adrianson
Proofreader: Gretchen Dykstra
Indexer: Valerie Perry
Cover Designer: Aren Howell Straiger
Interior Designer: Kim Scott
Compositor: Kim Scott

ISBN 13: 978-0-321-68368-7
ISBN 10: 0-321-68368-4

9 8 7 6 5 4 3 2 1

Printed and bound in the United States of America

For my wife, Rebecca Blood Garrett,
who makes all things possible.

Table of Contents

About the Author

Photo by: Colin Peck

Jesse James Garrett is one of the founders of Adaptive Path, a user experience consultancy based in San Francisco. Since 1995, Jesse has worked on Web projects for companies such as AT&T, Intel, Boeing, Motorola, Hewlett-Packard, and National Public Radio. His contributions to the field of user experience include the Visual Vocabulary, an open notation system for information architecture documentation that is now used by organizations around the world. His personal site at **www.jjg.net** is one of the Web's most popular destinations for information architecture resources, and he is a frequent speaker on information architecture and user experience issues.

Acknowledgements for the Second Edition

Michael Nolan spent years prodding me to do a second edition. His persistence—and his ingenuity in finally coming up with an offer I couldn't pass up—are the reasons it exists at all.

At New Riders, the team of Rose Weisburd, Tracey Croom, and Kim Scott kept me on track. Nancy Davis, Charlene Will, Hilal Sala, and Mimi Vitetta helped in making things go. Thanks also to Samantha Bailey and Karl Fast for their support.

My wife, Rebecca Blood Garrett, remains my first, last, and most trusted editor, advisor, and confidant.

New additions to the musical score this time around were Japancakes, Mono, Maserati, Tarentel, Sleeping People, Codes in the Clouds, and (especially) Explosions in the Sky. Very special thanks to Steve Scarborough of Maserati for musical guidance.

Acknowledgements for the First Edition

Don't let the number of names on the cover fool you—it takes a lot of people to make a book happen.

First, I have to thank my partners at Adaptive Path: Lane Becker, Janice Fraser, Mike Kuniavsky, Peter Merholz, Jeffrey Veen, and Indi Young. It is through their indulgence that I was able to take on this project at all.

Then there's everyone at New Riders, particularly Michael Nolan, Karen Whitehouse, Victoria Elzey, Deborah Hittel-Shoaf, John Rahm, and Jake McFarland. Their guidance was essential to this process.

Kim Scott and Aren Howell lent a keen eye and attention to detail to the design of this book. Their patience with suggestions from the author was especially laudable.

Molly Wright Steenson and David Hoffer provided invaluable insight in their review of my manuscript. Every author should be so lucky.

Jess McMullin turned out to be my toughest critic in many ways, and this book is immeasurably improved by his influence.

Thanks are also due to the more experienced authors who gave me advice on how to tackle a project like this and maintain my sanity: Jeffrey Veen (again), Mike Kuniavsky (again), Steve Krug, June Cohen, Nathan Shedroff, Louis Rosenfeld, Peter Morville, and (especially) Steve Champeon.

Others who offered valuable suggestions or simply good moral support included Lisa Chan, George Olsen, Christina Wodtke, Jessamyn West, Samantha Bailey, Eric Scheid, Michael Angeles, Javier Velasco, Antonio Volpon, Vuk Cosic, Thierry Goulet, and Dennis Woudt. They thought of things I didn't, and that makes them the best kind of colleagues.

Musical accompaniment for the writing process was provided by Man or Astro-man?, Pell Mell, Mermen, Dirty Three, Trans Am, Tortoise, Turing Machine, Don Caballero, Mogwai, Ui, Shadowy Men on a Shadowy Planet, Do Make Say Think, and (especially) Godspeed You Black Emperor!

Finally, there are three people without whom this book would never have happened: Dinah Sanders, who at a party one warm Texas night insisted there was someone I had to meet; my wife, Rebecca Blood, who makes me stronger and wiser in every way; and Daniel Grassam, without whose friendship, encouragement, and support I might not have found my way into this business at all. Thank you.

Introduction to the Second Edition

Let's cut to the chase: It's the second edition. What's different?

The main difference between this edition and the first is that this book is no longer just about Web sites. Yes, most of the examples are still Web-related, but overall, the themes, concepts, and principles apply to products and services of all kinds.

There are two reasons for this, both having to do with what's happened over the last ten years. One is what's happened to *Elements*, and one is what's happened to user experience itself.

Over the years, I've heard from (or heard about) people who have applied the *Elements* model to products that have nothing to do with the Web. In some cases they were Web designers asked to take on something new, like a mobile application. In other cases, they were designers of other kinds of products who somehow came across *Elements* and saw a connection to their own work.

Meanwhile, the field of user experience has broadened its horizons. Practitioners now regularly talk about the impact and value of user experience design in areas far beyond the limited context of the Web or even screen-based interactive applications that dominated the conversation back when this book was first written.

This new edition of the book takes a similarly broad view. The Web is still central to the book, if only to acknowledge the model's roots in that medium. But this book doesn't require an insider's knowledge of how Web development happens—so even if you don't create Web sites, you should be able to see how to apply these ideas in your own work.

Despite all this, those of you who have read the first edition should rest assured: This is not a radical reinvention. It's a honing and refinement of the familiar Elements model you know (and hopefully love), with the same core ideas and philosophy intact. The little things change, but the big ones really don't

I remain gratified and humbled by where people have taken *Elements*. I can't wait to see what happens next!

Jesse James Garrett
November 2010

Introduction to the First Edition

This is not a how-to book. There are many, many books out there that explain how Web sites get made. This is not one of them.

This is not a book about technology. There is not a single line of code to be found between these covers.

This is not a book of answers. Instead, this book is about asking the right questions.

This book will tell you what you need to know before you go read those other books. If you need the big picture, if you need to understand the context for the decisions that user experience practitioners make, this book is for you.

This book is designed to be read easily in just a few hours. If you're a newcomer to the world of user experience—maybe you're an executive responsible for hiring a user experience team, or maybe you're a writer or designer just finding your way into this field—this book will give you the foundation you need. If you're already familiar with the methods and concerns of the field of user experience, this book will help you communicate them more effectively to the people you work with.

The Story Behind the Book

Because I get asked about it a lot, here is the story of how *The Elements of User Experience* came to be.

In late 1999, I became the first information architect hired into a long-established Web design consultancy. In many ways, I was responsible for defining my position and educating people both about what I did, and how it fit in with what they did. Initially, they were perhaps cautious and a bit wary, but soon they came to recognize that I was there to make their jobs easier, not harder, and that my presence did not mean their authority was diminished.

Simultaneously, I was compiling a personal collection of online material related to my work. (This would eventually find its way onto the Web as my information architecture resources page at www.jjg.net/ia/.) While I was doing this research, I was continually frustrated by the seemingly arbitrary and random use of different terms for the basic concepts in the field. What one source called information design appeared to be the same as what another called information architecture. A third rolled everything together under interface design.

Over the course of late 1999 and January 2000, I struggled to arrive at a self-consistent set of definitions for these concerns and to find a way to express the relationships between them. But I was busy with actual paying work as well, and the model I was trying to formulate wasn't really working out anyway; so by the end of January I had given up on the whole idea.

That March I traveled to Austin, Texas, for the annual South by Southwest Interactive Festival. It was an engaging and thought-provoking week during which I didn't get much sleep—the conference's schedule of day and night activities begins to resemble a marathon after a couple of days.

At the end of that week, as I walked through the terminal of the airport in Austin preparing to board the plane back to San Francisco, it abruptly popped into my head: a three-dimensional matrix that captured all of my ideas. I waited patiently until we boarded the plane. As soon as I reached my seat, I pulled out a notebook and sketched it all out.

Upon my return to San Francisco, I was almost immediately laid up with an enervating head cold. I spent about a week sliding in and out of a fevered delirium. When I felt particularly lucid, I worked on turning my notebook sketch into a finished diagram that would fit neatly onto a letter-size piece of paper. I called it "The Elements of User Experience." Later I would hear about how, for many people, that title evoked memories of periodic tables and Strunk and White. Unfortunately, none of these associations was in my mind when I chose that title—I chose *elements* out of a thesaurus to replace the more awkward and technical-sounding *components*.

On March 30, I posted the final product on the Web. (It's still there; you can find the original diagram at www.jjg.net/ia/elements. pdf.) The diagram started getting some attention, first from Peter Merholz and Jeffrey Veen, who would later become my partners in Adaptive Path. Soon after, I spoke with more people about it at the first Information Architecture Summit. Eventually I started hearing from people all over the world about how they had used the diagram to educate their co-workers and to give their organizations a common vocabulary for discussing these issues.

In the year after it was first released, "The Elements of User Experience" was downloaded from my site more than 20,000 times. I began to hear about how it was being used in large organizations and tiny Web development groups to help them work and communicate more effectively. By this time, I was beginning to formulate the idea for a book that would address this need better than a single sheet of paper could.

Another March rolled around, and again I found myself in Austin for South by Southwest. There I met Michael Nolan of New Riders Publishing and told him my idea. He was enthusiastic about it, and fortunately, his bosses turned out to be as well.

Thus, as much by luck as by intent, this book found its way into your hands. I hope that what you do with the ideas presented here is as enlightening and rewarding for you as putting them together in this book has been for me.

Jesse James Garrett
July 2002

chapter 1

User Experience and Why It Matters

We have a double-edged relationship with the products and services we use. They empower us and frustrate us; they simplify and complicate our lives; they separate us and bring us closer together. But even though we interact with countless products and services every day, we easily forget that they are made by people, and that someone, somewhere should get the credit when they work well for us—or get the blame when they don't.

Everyday Miseries

Everyone, every once in a while, has one of those days.

You know the kind of day I'm talking about: You wake up to sunlight streaming in your window and wonder why your alarm clock hasn't gone off yet. You look over to see that your clock thinks it's 3:43 a.m. You stumble out of bed to find another clock, which tells you that you can still make it to work on time—if you leave in 10 minutes.

You turn on the coffeemaker and hustle to get dressed, but when you go to retrieve your dose of life-sustaining caffeine, there's no coffee in the pot. No time to figure out why—you've got to get to work!

You get about a block from your house when you realize that the car needs gas. At the gas station, you try to use the one pump that takes credit cards, but this time it won't accept yours. So you have to go inside and pay the cashier, but first you have to wait in line while the cashier very slowly helps everyone in front of you.

You have to take a detour because of a traffic accident, so the drive takes longer than you expected. It's official: Despite all your efforts, you are now late for work. Finally, you make it to your desk. You're agitated, harried, weary, and irritable—and your day hasn't even really started yet. And you still haven't had any coffee.

Introducing User Experience

It seems like a string of bad luck—just one of those days. But let's rewind that series of events, look closer, and see if, somehow, all that bad luck could have been avoided.

The accident: The accident on the road happened because the driver took his eyes off the road for a moment to turn the radio down. He had to look down because it was impossible to identify which was the volume control by touch alone.

The register: The line at the register in the gas station moved so slowly because the cash register was complex and confusing, and unless the clerk paid extra-close attention while ringing something up, he would make a mistake and have to start all over again. If the register had been simpler and the layout and colors of the buttons different, that line never would have formed.

The pump: You wouldn't have had to stand in that line at all if the pump had accepted your card. It would have done so if you had turned the card around the other way to swipe it, but nothing on the pump indicated which way the card should be turned, and you were in such a hurry that you didn't think to try every orientation.

The coffeemaker: The coffeemaker didn't make coffee because you didn't push down the power button all the way. The machine doesn't do anything to let you know that it has been turned on: no light, no sound, no resistance you can feel when the button makes contact. You thought you had turned it on, but you were wrong. The problem could have been avoided altogether if you had set the coffeemaker to start brewing automatically first thing in the morning, but you never learned how to use that function—if you knew it existed at all. The display on the front is still blinking 12:00.

The clock: And now we come to the factor that started the whole chain of events: the alarm clock. The alarm didn't go off because the time was wrong. The time was wrong because your cat stepped on the clock in the middle of the night and reset it for you. (If this sounds implausible to you, don't laugh—it has happened to me. I have had to go to surprising lengths to find a clock that is impervious to cat meddling.) A slightly different configuration of buttons would have prevented the cat from resetting the clock, and consequently you would have been out of bed with plenty of time—no need to rush at all.

In short, every one of the previous cases of "bad luck" could have been avoided had someone made different choices in designing a product or service. These examples all demonstrate a lack of attention to the **user experience**: the experience the product creates for the people who use it in the real world. When a product is being developed, people pay a great deal of attention to what it does. User experience is the other, often overlooked, side of the equation— how it works—that can often make the difference between a successful product and a failure.

User experience is not about the inner workings of a product or service. User experience is about how it works on the outside, where a person comes into contact with it. When someone asks you what it's like to use a product or service, they're asking about the user experience. Is it hard to do simple things? Is it easy to figure out? How does it feel to interact with the product?

That interaction often involves pushing a lot of buttons, as in the case of technology products such as alarm clocks, coffeemakers, or cash registers. Sometimes, it's just a matter of a simple physical mechanism, such as the gas cap on your car. However, every product that is used by someone creates a user experience: books, ketchup bottles, reclining armchairs, cardigan sweaters.

For any kind of product or service, it's the little things that count. Having a button click when you push it down doesn't seem like much, but when that click makes the difference between getting coffee and not getting coffee, it matters a great deal. Even if you never realized that the design of that button was causing you trouble, how would you feel about a coffeemaker that you were able to use successfully only part of the time? How would you feel about the manufacturer? Would you buy another product from that company in the future? Probably not. Thus, for the want of a button that clicks, a customer is lost.

From Product Design to User Experience Design

~~When most people think about product design~~ (if they think about product design at all), ~~they often think of it in terms of aesthetic appeal:~~ a well-designed product is one that looks good to the eye and feels good to the touch. (The senses of smell and taste don't come into play for most products. Sound is often overlooked but can be an important part of the aesthetic appeal of a product.) Whether it's the curve of a sports car's body or the texture of a power drill's grip, the aesthetic dimension of product design is a sure attention-getter.

~~Another common way people think about product design is in functional terms:~~ A well-designed product is one that does what it promises to do. And a badly designed product is one that somehow doesn't: scissors that don't cut even though the blades are sharp, a pen that doesn't write even though it's full of ink, a printer that constantly jams.

All of these can certainly be failures of design. These products might look great and work well functionally, but designing products with the user experience as an explicit outcome means looking beyond the functional or aesthetic.

Some people responsible for creating products may not think in terms of design at all. For them, the process of creating a product is about development: steadily building up and refining the features and functions of the product until they add up to something viable in the marketplace.

In this view, the design of the product is dictated by its functionality—or, as designers sometimes put it, "form follows function." This approach makes complete sense for the inner workings of a product, the parts concealed from a user. But when it comes to the parts of a product that are user-facing—the buttons, displays, labels, and so forth—the "correct" form isn't dictated by functionality at all. Instead, it's dictated by the psychology and behavior of the users themselves.

User experience design often deals with questions of context. Aesthetic design makes sure the button on the coffeemaker is an appealing shape and texture. Functional design makes sure it triggers the appropriate action on the device. User experience design makes sure the aesthetic and functional aspects of the button work in the context of the rest of the product, asking questions like, "Is the button too small for such an important function?" User experience design also makes sure the button works in the context of what the user is trying to accomplish, asking questions like, "Is the button in the right place relative to the other controls the user would be using at the same time?"

Designing (for) Experience: Use Matters

What's the difference between designing a product and designing a user experience? After all, every product intended for humans has a user, and every time a product is used, it delivers an experience. Consider a simple product such as a chair or a table. To use the chair you sit on it; to use the table you place other objects on it. In both cases, the product can fail to deliver a satisfactory experience: if the chair won't support the weight of a person, for example, or the table is unsteady.

But the manufacturers of chairs and tables tend not to employ user experience designers. In these simple cases, the requirements to deliver a successful user experience are built into the definition of the product itself: In some sense, a chair you can't sit on isn't a chair at all.

With more complex products, though, the requirements to deliver a successful user experience are independent of the definition of the product. A telephone is defined by its ability to place and/or receive calls; but there are practically infinite variations on the telephone that can deliver on this basic definition—with widely varying degrees of successful user experience.

And the more complex a product is, the more difficult it becomes to identify exactly how to deliver a successful experience to the user. Each additional feature, function, or step in the process of using a product creates another opportunity for the experience to fall short. A modern mobile phone has many, many more functions than a desk phone of, say, the 1950s. As a result, the process of creating a successful product has to be quite different. That's where product design has to be supported by user experience design.

User Experience and the Web

User experience is vital to all kinds of products and services. This book is primarily about the user experience of one particular kind of product: Web sites. (I'm using the term *site* here to refer to both content-oriented Web products and interactive Web applications.)

On the Web, user experience becomes even more important than it is for other kinds of products. But the lessons we've learned from creating user experiences on the Web can be applied far beyond its boundaries.

Web sites are complicated pieces of technology, and something funny happens when people have trouble using complicated pieces of technology: They blame themselves. They feel like they must have done something wrong. They feel like they weren't paying enough attention. They feel stupid. Sure, it's irrational. After all, it's not their fault the site doesn't work the way they expect it to. But they feel stupid anyway. And if you intend to drive people away from your site (or any product), it's hard to imagine a more effective approach than making them feel stupid when they use it.

Regardless of the type of site, in virtually every case, a Web site is a self-service product. There is no instruction manual to read beforehand, no training seminar to attend, no customer service representative to help guide the user through the site. There is only the user, facing the site alone with only her wits and personal experience to guide her.

Faced with a wide array of choices, the user is left to her own devices to determine which features of a site will meet her needs.

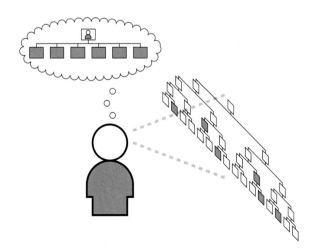

It's bad enough that she's been stuck in the position of having to figure out the site on her own. The fact that most sites don't even acknowledge her helpless condition only makes matters worse. Despite the vital strategic importance of user experience to the success of a Web site, the simple matter of understanding what people want and need has been a low priority for most of the history of the medium.

If user experience is such a vital part of any Web site, why is it so often neglected in the development process? Many Web sites are built with the idea that being first to market is the key to success. In the earliest days of the Web, sites like Yahoo! built early leads that later competitors struggled to overcome. Established companies raced to set up Web sites, determined not to be perceived as falling behind the times. But in most cases, companies considered merely having deployed the site a great accomplishment; whether the site actually worked for people was, at best, an afterthought.

To gain market share against these first-movers, competitors often add more and more content and functionality in hopes of drawing in new customers (and maybe stealing a few customers from the competition). This race to cram more features into products is hardly unique to the Web; from wristwatches to mobile phones, featuritis is endemic to many product categories.

Having more features, however, turns out to be only a temporary source of competitive advantage. With the added complexity that comes with an ever-expanding feature set, sites become increasingly unwieldy, hard to use, and unappealing to the very first-timers they are supposed to draw in. And still, many organizations pay little attention to what users like, find valuable, or are really able to use.

More and more businesses have now come to recognize that providing a quality user experience is an essential, sustainable competitive advantage—not just for Web sites, but for all kinds of products and services. It is user experience that forms the customer's impression of a company's offerings; it is user experience that differentiates a company from its competitors; and it is user experience that determines whether your customer will ever come back.

Good User Experience Is Good Business

Maybe you don't sell anything on your site. All you provide is information about your company. It might seem that you have a monopoly on that information—if people want it, they have to get it from you. You don't have competition in the same way that an online bookstore does. Nevertheless, you can't afford to neglect the user experience of your site.

If your site consists mainly of what Web pros call *content*—that is, information—then one of the main goals of your site is to communicate that information as effectively as possible. It's not enough just to put it out there. It has to be presented in a way that helps people absorb it and understand it. Otherwise, the user might not ever find out that you offer the service or product they're looking for. And even if they do manage to find that information, they're likely to draw the conclusion that if your site is difficult to work with, your company probably is as well.

Even if your site is a Web-based application that people can use to accomplish certain tasks (like buying airplane tickets or managing bank accounts), effective communication is a key factor in the success of your product. The world's most powerful functionality falters and fails if users can't figure out how to make it work.

Simply put, if your users have a bad experience, they won't come back. If they have an OK experience with your site but a better experience with your competitor's site, they'll go back to that competitor, not you. Features and functions always matter, but user experience has a far greater effect on customer loyalty. All your sophisticated technology and brand messaging won't bring those customers back a second time. A good user experience will—and you don't get much of a second chance to get it right.

Customer loyalty isn't the only way that focusing on the user experience of your site can pay off. Businesses with an eye on the bottom line want to know about the **return on investment**, or ROI. ROI is usually measured in terms of money: For every dollar you spend, how many dollars of value are you getting back? That's the ROI. But return on investment does not have to be expressed in strictly monetary terms. All you need is a measurement that shows that your money going out translates into value for your company.

One common measure of return on investment is **conversion rate**. Any time you want to encourage your customers to take the next step in building a relationship with you—whether that involves something as complex as customizing the site to their preferences or as simple as signing up to receive an e-mail newsletter—there's a conversion rate you can measure. By keeping track of what percentage of users you convert to the next level, you can measure how effectively your site is meeting your business goals.

Conversion rate is a common way of measuring the effectiveness of a user experience.

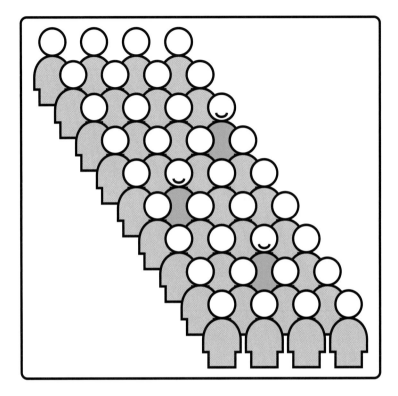

3 subscription sign-ups

÷

36 visitors

=

8.33% conversion rate

Conversion rate becomes even more important in the case of commerce sites. Far more people browse a commerce site than buy from it. A quality user experience is a key factor in converting these casual browsers into active buyers. Even a tiny increase in your conversion rate can translate into a dramatic leap in revenue. It's not uncommon for a change in conversion rate as small as one-tenth of one percent to result in a revenue increase of ten percent or more.

On any site where users have the opportunity to give you some money, you have a measurable conversion rate, whether you're selling books, cat food, or subscriptions to the content of the site itself. Conversion rate can give you a better sense of the return on your user experience investment than simple sales figures. Sales can suffer if you're not successful in getting the word out about your site. Conversion rate tracks how successful you are in getting those who visit to spend some money.

Even if your site doesn't lend itself readily to an ROI metric like conversion rate, that doesn't mean the effect of user experience on your business is any less significant. Whether they are used by your customers, your partners, or your employees, Web sites can have all kinds of indirect effects on the bottom line.

No one outside your company might ever see the site you run (as in the case of an internal tool or an intranet), but the user experience still makes a huge difference. Often, it can mean the difference between a project that creates value for the organization and a project that becomes a resource-consuming nightmare.

Any user experience effort aims to improve efficiency. This basically comes in two key forms: helping people work faster and helping them make fewer mistakes. Improving the efficiency of the tools you use improves the productivity of the business as a whole. The less time it takes to complete any given task, the more you can get done in a day. In keeping with the old notion that time is money, saving your employees time translates directly into saving your business money.

Efficiency doesn't only affect the bottom line, though. People like their jobs more when their tools are natural and easy to use, not frustrating and needlessly complex. If that person is you, these kinds of tools make the difference between coming home satisfied at the end of the day and coming home exhausted and hating your job. (Or at least, if you are coming home exhausted, it's for the right reasons—not because you've been struggling with your tools.)

Technology products that don't work the way people expect make them feel stupid—even if they ultimately accomplish what they set out to do.

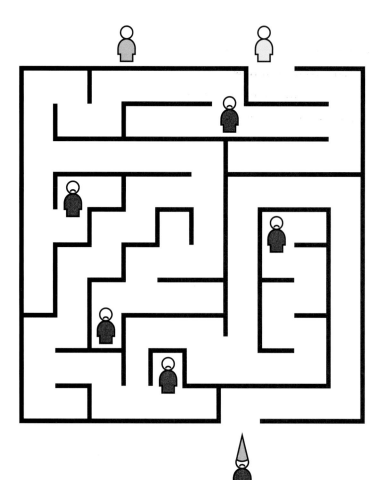

If that person is your employee, providing these kinds of tools increases not only their productivity, but also their job satisfaction, making the employee less likely to seek a new job. This, in turn, means you save on recruiting and training costs, plus you benefit from the higher level of quality that a more dedicated, experienced employee brings to her work.

Minding Your Users

The practice of creating engaging, efficient user experiences is called **user-centered design**. The concept of user-centered design is very simple: Take the user into account every step of the way as you develop your product. The implications of this simple concept, however, are surprisingly complex.

Everything the user experiences should be the result of a conscious decision on your part. Realistically, you might have to make a compromise here and there because of the time or expense involved in creating a better solution. But a user-centered design process ensures that those compromises don't happen by accident. By thinking about the user experience, breaking it down into its component elements, and looking at it from several perspectives, you can ensure that you know all the ramifications of your decisions.

The biggest reason user experience should matter to you is that it matters to your users. If you don't provide them with a positive experience, they won't use your product. And without users, all you've got is a dusty Web server (or warehouse full of products) somewhere, idly waiting to fulfill a request that will never come. For the users who do come, you must set out to provide them with an experience that is cohesive, intuitive, and maybe even pleasurable—an experience in which everything works the way it should. No matter how the rest of their day has gone.

chapter **2**

Meet the Elements

The user experience design process is all about ensuring that no aspect of the user's experience with your product happens without your conscious, explicit intent. This means taking into account every possibility of every action the user is likely to take and understanding the user's expectations at every step of the way through that process. It sounds like a big job, and in some ways it is. But by breaking the job of crafting the user experience down into its component elements, we can better understand the task as a whole.

The Five Planes

Most people, at one time or another, have purchased a physical product over the Web. The experience is pretty much the same every time: You go to the site, you find the item you want (maybe by using a search engine or maybe by browsing a catalog), you give the site your credit card number and your address, and the site confirms that the product will be shipped to you.

That neat, tidy experience actually results from a whole set of decisions—some small, some large—about how the site looks, how it behaves, and what it allows you to do. These decisions build upon each other, informing and influencing all aspects of the user experience. If we peel away the layers of that experience, we can begin to understand how those decisions are made.

The Surface Plane

On the **surface** you see a series of Web pages, made up of images and text. Some of these images are things you can click on, performing some sort of function such as taking you to a shopping cart. Some of these images are just illustrations, such as a photograph of a product for sale or the logo of the site itself.

The Skeleton Plane

Beneath that surface is the **skeleton** of the site: the placement of buttons, controls, photos, and blocks of text. The skeleton is designed to optimize the arrangement of these elements for maximum effect and efficiency—so that you remember the logo and can find that shopping cart button when you need it.

The Structure Plane

The skeleton is a concrete expression of the more abstract **structure** of the site. The skeleton might define the placement of the interface elements on our checkout page; the structure would define how users got to that page and where they could go when they were finished there. The skeleton might define the arrangement of navigational elements allowing the users to browse categories of products; the structure would define what those categories were.

The Scope Plane

The structure defines the way in which the various features and functions of the site fit together. Just what those features and functions are constitutes the **scope** of the site. For example, some commerce sites offer a feature that enables users to save previously used shipping addresses so they can be used again. Whether that feature—or any feature—is included on a site is a question of scope.

The Strategy Plane

The scope is fundamentally determined by the **strategy** of the site. This strategy incorporates not only what the people running the site want to get out of it but what the users want to get out of the site as well. In the case of our store example, some of the strategic objectives are pretty obvious: Users want to buy products, and we want to sell them. Other objectives—such as the role that advertising or content produced by our users plays in our business model, for example—might not be so easy to articulate.

Building from Bottom to Top

These five planes—strategy, scope, structure, skeleton, and surface—provide a conceptual framework for talking about user experience problems and the tools we use to solve them.

On each plane, the issues we must deal with become a little less abstract and a little more concrete. On the lowest plane, we are not concerned with the final shape of the site, product, or service at all—we only care about how the site will fit into our strategy (while meeting the needs of our users). On the highest plane, we are only concerned with the most concrete details of the appearance of the product. Plane by plane, the decisions we have to make become a little more specific and involve finer levels of detail.

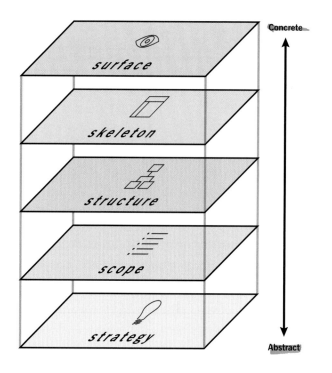

Each plane is dependent on the planes below it. So, the surface depends on the skeleton, which depends on the structure, which depends on the scope, which depends on the strategy. When the choices we make don't align with those above and below, projects derail, deadlines are missed, and costs begin to skyrocket as the development team tries to piece together components that don't naturally fit. Even worse, when the product finally does launch, users often hate it, because it doesn't deliver a satisfying experience. This dependence means that decisions on the strategy plane will have a sort of "ripple effect" all the way up the chain. Conversely, the choices available to us on each plane are constrained by the decisions we make about issues on the planes below it.

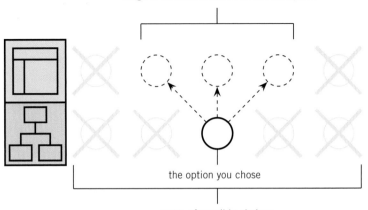

range of choices available on the next plane

the option you chose

range of possible choices

The choices you make on each plane affect the choices available to you on the next plane above it.

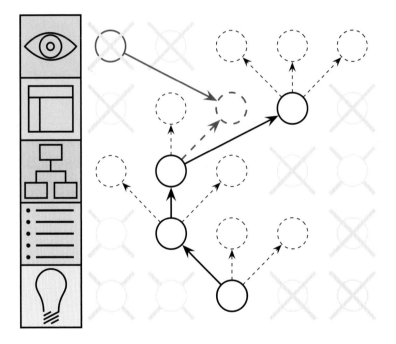

This ripple effect means that choosing an "out of bounds" option on an upper plane will require rethinking decisions on lower planes.

That does not mean, however, that every decision about a lower plane must be made before the plane above it can be addressed. Dependencies run in both directions, with decisions made on upper planes sometimes forcing a reevaluation (or an evaluation made for the first time!) of issues on lower planes. At each level, we make decisions according to what the competition is doing, industry best practices, what we know about our users, and plain old common sense. These decisions can have a ripple effect in both directions.

Requiring work on each plane to **finish** before work on the next can **start** leads to unsatisfactory results for you and your users.

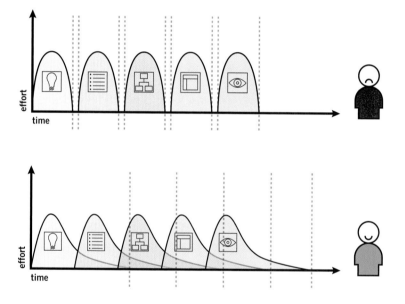

A better approach is to have work on each plane **finish** before work on the next can **finish**.

If you consider your decisions on lower planes to be set in stone before you take on your decisions on higher planes, you will almost certainly be throwing your project schedule—and possibly the success of your final product—into jeopardy.

Instead, you should plan your project so that work on any plane cannot *finish* before work on lower planes has finished. The important consideration here is to not build the roof of the house before you know the shape of its foundation.

A Basic Duality

Of course, there are more than just five elements of user experience, and as with any specialized field, this one has evolved a vocabulary all its own. To someone encountering the field for the first time, user experience can appear to be a complicated business. All these seemingly identical terms are thrown around: interaction design, information design, information architecture. What do they mean? Anything? Or are they just more meaningless industry buzzwords?

To further complicate matters, people will use the same terms in different ways. One person might use "information design" to refer to what another knows as "information architecture." And what's the difference between "interface design" and "interaction design?" Is there one?

When the Web started, it was all about information. People could create documents, and they could link them to other documents. Tim Berners-Lee, the inventor of the Web, created it as a way for researchers in the high-energy physics community, who were spread out all over the world, to share and refer to each other's findings. He knew the Web had the potential to be much more than that, but few others really understood how great its potential was.

People originally seized on the Web as a new publishing medium, but as technology advanced and new features were added to Web browsers and Web servers alike, the Web took on new functional capabilities. After the Web began to catch on in the larger Internet community, it developed a more complex and robust feature set that would enable Web sites not only to distribute information but to collect and manipulate it as well. With this, the Web became more interactive, responding to the input of users in ways that built upon and sometimes moved beyond traditional desktop applications.

With the advent of commercial interests on the Web, this application functionality found a wide range of uses, such as electronic commerce, social media, and financial services, among others. Meanwhile, the Web continued to flourish as a publishing medium, with countless newspaper and magazine sites augmenting the wave of Web-only blogs and "e-zines" being published. Technology continued to advance on both fronts as all kinds of sites made the transition from static collections of information that changed infrequently to dynamic, database-driven sites that were constantly evolving.

When the Web user experience community started to form, its members spoke two different languages. One group saw every problem as an application design problem, and applied problem-solving approaches from the traditional desktop and mainframe software worlds. (These, in turn, were rooted in common practices applied to creating all kinds of products, from cars to running shoes.) The other group saw the Web in terms of information distribution and retrieval, and applied problem-solving approaches from the traditional worlds of publishing, media, and information science.

This became quite a stumbling block. Very little progress could be made when the community could not even agree on basic terminology. The waters were further muddied by the fact that most Web sites could not be neatly categorized as either functional applications or information resources—a huge number seemed to be a sort of hybrid, incorporating qualities from each world.

To address this basic duality in the nature of the Web, let's split our five planes down the middle. On the left, we'll put those elements specific to the Web as a platform for **functionality**. On the right, we'll put the elements specific to the Web as an **information medium**.

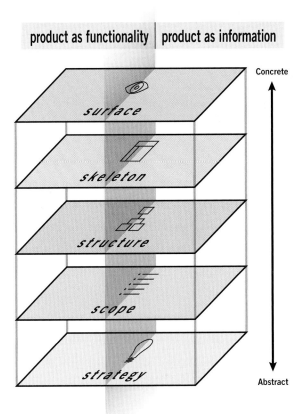

On the functionality side, we are mainly concerned with **tasks**—the steps involved in a process and how people think about completing them. Here, we consider the product as a tool or set of tools that the user employs to accomplish one or more tasks.

On the opposite side, our concern is what **information** the product offers and what it means to our users. Creating an information-rich user experience is about enabling people to find, absorb, and make sense of the information we provide.

The Elements of User Experience

Now we can map that whole confusing array of terms into the model. By breaking each plane down into its component elements, we'll be able to take a closer look at how all the pieces fit together in the course of designing the whole user experience.

The Strategy Plane

The same strategic concerns come into play for both functionality-oriented products and information-oriented resources. **User needs** are the goals for the site that come from outside our organization—specifically from the people who will use our site. We must understand what our audience wants from us and how that fits in with other goals they have.

Balanced against user needs are our own objectives for the site. These **product objectives** can be business goals ("Make $1 million in sales over the Web this year") or other kinds of goals ("Inform voters about the candidates in the next election"). In Chapter 3 we'll go into more detail about these elements.

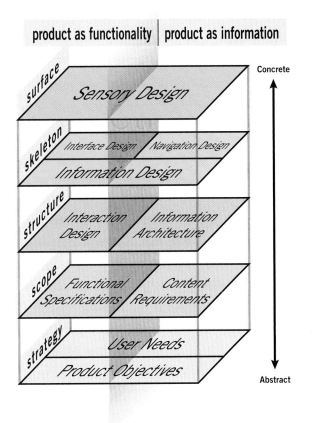

The Scope Plane

On the functionality side, the strategy is translated into scope through the creation of functional specifications: a detailed description of the "feature set" of the product. On the information side, scope takes the form of **content requirements**: a description of the various content elements that will be required. Chapter 4 will cover the scope elements.

The Structure Plane

The scope is given structure on the functionality side through **interaction design,** in which we define how the system behaves in response to the user. For information resources, the structure is the **information architecture**: the arrangement of content elements to facilitate human understanding. You'll find more details on these in Chapter 5.

The Skeleton Plane

The skeleton plane breaks down into three components. On both sides, we must address **information design**: the presentation of information in a way that facilitates understanding. For functionality-oriented products, the skeleton also includes **interface design,** or arranging interface elements to enable users to interact with the functionality of the system. The interface for an information resource is its **navigation design**: the set of screen elements that allow the user to move through the information architecture. There's more about the skeleton plane in Chapter 6.

The Surface Plane

Finally, we have the surface. Regardless of whether we are dealing with a functionality-oriented product or an information resource, our concern here is the same: the **sensory experience** created by the finished product. It's trickier than it sounds; you can find out all about it in Chapter 7.

Using the Elements

This model, divided up into neat boxes and planes, is a convenient way to think about user experience problems. In reality, of course, the lines between these areas are not so clearly drawn. Frequently, it can be difficult to identify whether a particular user experience problem is best solved through attention to one element instead of another. Can a change to the visuals do the trick, or will the underlying navigation design have to be reworked? Some problems require attention in several areas at once, and some seem to straddle the borders identified in this model.

Few products or services fall exclusively on one side of this model or the other. Within each plane, the elements must work together to accomplish that plane's goals. Separating the effects of decisions you make about one element from all other elements on the plane is very difficult. For example, information design, navigation design, and interface design jointly define the skeleton of a product. All the elements on every plane have a common function in determining the larger user experience—in this case, defining the product's skeleton—even if they perform that function in different ways.

The way organizations delegate responsibility for user experience issues often complicates matters further. In some organizations, you will encounter people with job titles like information architect or interface designer. Don't be confused by this. These people generally have expertise spanning many of the elements of user experience, not just the specialty indicated by their title. It's not necessary to have a member of your team who is a specialist in each of these areas; instead, you only have to ensure that someone spends at least part of their time thinking about each of these issues.

A couple of additional factors go into shaping the final user experience that you won't find covered in detail here. The first of these is **content**. The old saying (well, old in Web years) is that "content is king" on the Web. This is absolutely true—the single most important thing most Web sites can offer to their users is content that those users will find valuable.

Users don't visit Web sites to experience the joy of navigation. The content that is available to you (or that you have resources to obtain and manage) will play a huge role in shaping your site. In the case of an online store, we might decide that we want the users to be able to see cover images of all the books we sell. If we can get them, will we have a way to catalog them, keep track of them, and keep them up to date? And what if we can't get photos of the book covers at all? These content questions are essential to the ultimate user experience of the site.

Second, **technology** can be just as important as content in creating a successful user experience. In many cases, the nature of the experience you can provide your users is largely determined by technology. In the early days of the Web, the tools to connect Web sites to databases were fairly primitive and limited. As the technology has advanced, however, databases have become more widely used to drive Web sites. This in turn has enabled more and more sophisticated user experience approaches, such as dynamic navigation systems that change in response to the way users move through the site. Technology is always changing, and the field of user experience always has to adapt to it. Nevertheless, the fundamental elements of user experience remain the same.

Although I developed the Elements model in the course of my work on Web sites, others have since applied it to a wide range of products and services. If you work on the Web, everything in this book applies to you. If you work on other kinds of technology products, you'll see strong parallels to familiar considerations. Even if you work on products or services that have nothing to do with technology, you can map these concepts to your own processes.

The rest of this book looks at these elements, plane by plane, in greater detail. We'll take a closer look at some of the tools and techniques commonly used to address each element. Along the way, we'll see how these elements come into play in products that aren't Web sites at all. We'll see what the elements on each plane have in common, what makes each one different, and how they affect each other to help us create the total user experience.

chapter **3**

The Strategy Plane

Product Objectives and User Needs

The foundation of a successful user experience is a clearly articulated strategy. Knowing both what we want the product to accomplish for our organization and what we want it to accomplish for our users informs the decisions we have to make about every aspect of the user experience. But answering these simple questions can be trickier than it looks.

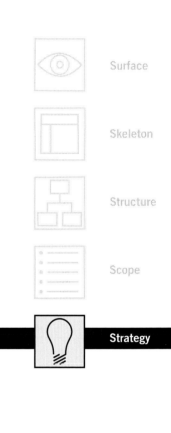

Surface

Skeleton

Structure

Scope

Strategy

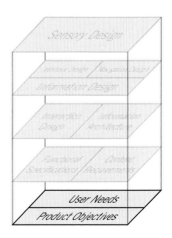

Defining the Strategy

The most common reason for the failure of a Web site is not technology. It's not user experience either. Web sites most often fail because—before the first line of code was written, the first pixel was pushed, or the first server was installed—nobody bothered to answer two very basic questions:

▶ What do we want to get out of this product?

▶ What do our users want to get out of it?

product as functionality | product as information

scope

strategy

User Needs

Product Objectives

By answering the first question, we describe the **product objectives** coming from inside the organization. The second question addresses **user needs**, objectives imposed on the product from outside. Together, product objectives and user needs form the strategy plane, the foundation for every decision in our process as we design the user experience. Yet, amazingly, many user experience projects do not begin with a clear, explicit understanding of the underlying strategy.

The key word here is *explicit*. The more clearly we can articulate exactly what we want, and exactly what others want from us, the more precisely we can adjust our choices to meet these goals.

Product Objectives

The first part of making our strategy explicit is examining our own objectives for the product or service. Too often, product objectives exist only as an unspoken understanding among those building the product. When that understanding remains unspoken, different people often have different ideas about what the product is supposed to accomplish.

Business Goals

People commonly use terms like *business goals* or *business drivers* to describe internal strategic objectives. I'm going to use the term *product objectives* because these other terms are both too narrow and too broad: Too narrow because not every internal goal is a business goal (after all, not every organization has the same kinds of goals that businesses do), and too broad because our concern here really is to identify in the most specific terms possible what we expect the product itself to accomplish, regardless of the rest of our business activities.

Most people start out describing objectives for their products in very general terms. In the case of Web sites, they fundamentally serve one of two purposes: to make the company money or to save the company money. Sometimes it's both. But exactly how these sites are supposed to do that is not always clear.

On the other hand, objectives that are too specific don't adequately describe the strategic concerns at issue. For example, stating that one of your objectives is "to provide users with a real-time text communications tool" doesn't explain how such a tool helps advance the objectives of your organization, or how it helps meet the needs of your users.

In trying to strike a balance between being too specific and being too general, we want to avoid jumping ahead to identify solutions when we don't yet fully understand the problems. To create a successful user experience, we have to make sure that every decision we make is rooted in a firm understanding of its consequences. Clearly defining the conditions for success—without defining the path to get there—assures that we don't get ahead of ourselves.

Brand Identity

One essential consideration in formulating the objectives for any product is brand identity. When most of us see the word *branding*, we think of things like logos, color palettes, and typography. While these visual aspects of brand are important (we'll revisit them in more detail when we get to the surface plane in Chapter 7), the concept of brand extends far beyond the visual. Brand identity—a set of conceptual associations or emotional reactions—is important because it's inescapable. In the minds of your users, an impression about your organization is inevitably created by their interactions with your product.

You must choose whether that impression happens by accident or as a result of conscious choices you have made in designing your product. Most organizations choose to exert some control over the perception of their brand, which is why communicating brand identity is a very common product objective. Branding isn't just for commercial entities either—every organization with a Web site, from nonprofit foundations to government agencies to individuals, creates an impression through user experience. By codifying the specific qualities of that impression as an explicit objective, you increase your chances that it will be a positive impression.

Success Metrics

Races have finish lines. An important part of understanding your objectives is understanding how you will know when you have reached them.

These are known as **success metrics**: indicators we can track after the product has been launched to see whether it is meeting our own objectives and our users' needs. Defining good success metrics not only influences decisions made over the course of the project; achieving them provides concrete evidence of the value of user experience efforts if you find yourself facing a skeptical audience when seeking budget approval for your next user experience project.

Sometimes these metrics are related to the product itself and how it is used. How much time does the average user spend on your site during each visit? (Analytics tools can help you determine this.) If you want to encourage your users to feel comfortable with the site, hang out, and explore what you have to offer, you'll want to see the time per visit increase. On the other hand, if you want to provide quick, get-in-get-out access to information and functionality, you may want to decrease the time per visit.

Success metrics are concrete indicators of how effectively the user experience is meeting strategic goals. In this example, measuring the number of visits per registered user per month indicates how valuable the site is to its core audience.

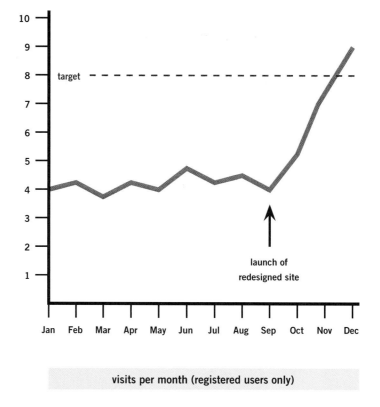

visits per month (registered users only)

For sites that depend on advertising revenue, impressions—the number of times each day an ad is served to a user—is an incredibly important metric. But you have to be careful to balance your objectives and the needs of your users. Adding several layers of navigational pages between the home page and the content users want will definitely increase your ad impressions, but is it serving user needs? Probably not. And in the long run, it will show: As your users get frustrated and decide not to come back, your impressions will drop from that initial high and will probably end up lower than they were when you started.

Not all success metrics have to be derived directly from your site. You can measure the indirect effects of the site as well. If your site provides solutions to common problems people encounter with your product, the number of phone calls coming into your customer support lines should go down. An effective intranet can provide ready access to tools and resources that can cut down on the time it takes for your salespeople to close a sale—which, in turn, translates directly into increased revenue.

For success metrics to meaningfully drive user experience decisions, those metrics must be clearly tied to aspects of user behavior that can be shaped by our design choices. Of course, when a redesign launches and daily revenue from online transactions jumps 40 percent, it's easy to see the relationship between cause and effect. But for changes that happen over a longer period of time, it can be difficult to identify whether those changes stem from the user experience or from other factors.

For example, the user experience of your site can't do much by itself to bring new users to your site—you'll have to rely upon word-of-mouth or your marketing efforts for that. But the user experience has a whole lot of influence on whether those visitors come back. Measuring return visits can be a great way to assess whether you're meeting user needs, but be careful: Sometimes those users don't come back because your competitor launched a gigantic advertising campaign or because your company just got some bad press. Any metric viewed in isolation can be misleading; be sure to take a step back and look at what's going on beyond the Web site to make sure you're getting the whole story.

User Needs

It can be easy to fall into the trap of thinking that we are designing our product or service for one idealized user—someone exactly like us. But we aren't designing for ourselves; we're designing for other people, and if those other people are going to like and use what we create, we need to understand who they are and what they need. By spending time researching those needs, we can break out of our own limited perspective and see the site from the point of view of the users.

Identifying user needs is complicated because users can be quite diverse. Even if we're creating a Web site for use inside our organization, we still may have to address a wide range of needs. If we are creating a mobile app intended for a consumer audience, the possibilities increase exponentially.

To get to the bottom of those needs, we have to define just who our users are. Once we know whom we're trying to reach, we can conduct research with them—in other words, ask them questions and observe their behavior. That research can help us define and prioritize what people need when they use our product.

User Segmentation

We can break this mass of user needs down into manageable chunks through **user segmentation**. We divide our audience into smaller groups (or segments) consisting of users with certain key characteristics in common. There are nearly as many ways to segment user groups as there are types of users, but here are a couple of the most common approaches.

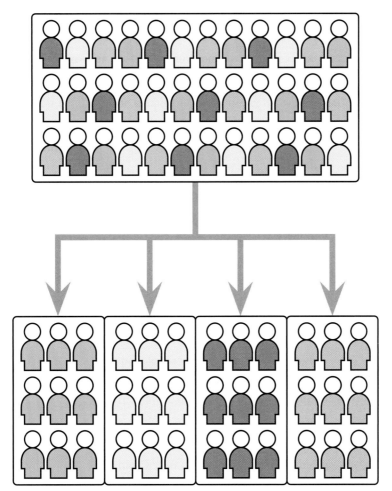

User segmentation
helps us understand
user needs better by
dividing the entire
audience into smaller
groups of people with
shared needs.

Market researchers commonly create audience segments based on
demographic criteria: gender, age, education level, marital status,
income, and so on. These demographic profiles can be quite general
(men 18–49) or very specific (unmarried, college-educated women
25–34 making over $50,000 a year).

Demographics aren't the only way you can look at your users. **Psychographic** profiles describe the attitudes and perceptions that your users have about the world or about the subject matter of your site in particular. Psychographics often correlate strongly with demographics: People in the same age group, location, and income level often have similar attitudes. But in many cases, demographically identical people have very different ways of seeing and interacting with the world. (Just think of everybody you went to high school with.) That's why uncovering the psychographics of your users can give you insights you can't get from demographics.

When developing a Web site or any technology product, there's another very important set of attitudes to consider: the users' attitudes toward the Web and technology itself. How much time do your users spend using the Web every week? Is technology a part of their daily lives? Do they like working with technology products? Do they always have the latest and greatest products, or do they only upgrade when they have to? Technophobes and power users approach Web sites in very different ways, and our designs need to accommodate them. Answers to questions like these can help us do just that.

In addition to understanding our users' familiarity and comfort level with technology, we need to understand what and how much they know about the subject matter of our site. Selling cookware to people just learning their way around a kitchen must be handled very differently from selling to professional cooks. Similarly, a stock-trading application used by those unfamiliar with the stock market will require a different approach from one for seasoned investors. These differences in experience or expertise can form the basis for segmenting our audience.

The way people use information often depends on their social or professional role. The information needs of the parents of a student applying for college are different from those of the student herself. Identifying the different roles of your product's users can help you separate them and analyze their different needs.

After you've conducted some research on your user groups, you might need to revise the segments you are working with. For example, if you're researching 25–34-year-old, college-educated women, you might find that the needs of the 30–34-year-olds differ from those of the 25–29 age group. If the difference is great enough, you might want to treat these as separate groups, rather than the single 25–34 group you started with. On the other hand, if the 18–24 group seems pretty similar to the 25–34 group, maybe you can combine them. Creating user segments is just a means to the end of uncovering user needs. You really only need as many different segments as you have different sets of user needs.

There's another important reason to create user segments: Not only will different groups of users have different needs, but sometimes those needs will be in direct opposition. Take the preceding example of the stock-trading application. The novices would probably be best served by an application that broke the process down into a sequence of simple steps. For the experts, however, such a sequence would be a hindrance. The experts need a unified interface that provides rapid access to a wide range of functions.

Obviously, we can't meet both sets of user needs with a single solution. Our options at this point are to focus on one user segment to the exclusion of the other, or to provide two separate ways for users to approach the same task. Whichever course we choose, this strategic decision will have consequences for every additional choice we make about the user experience.

Usability and User Research

To understand what our users need, we first have to get a sense of who they are. The field of **user research** is devoted to collecting the data needed to develop that understanding.

Some research tools—such as surveys, interviews, or focus groups—are best suited for gathering information about the general attitudes and perceptions of your users. Other research tools—such as user tests or field studies—are more appropriate for understanding specific aspects of user behavior and interaction with your product.

Generally, the more time you spend with each individual user, the more detailed the information you will get from the research study. However, that additional time spent with each user necessarily means you won't be able to include as many users in the study (if only because the product or service has to launch eventually).

Market research methods like surveys and focus groups can be valuable sources of general information about your users. These methods are most effective when you clearly articulate for yourself what information you're trying to get out of them. Do you want to find out what your users are doing when they use a particular feature of your product? Or maybe you already know that, but you need to know why they're doing it. The more clearly you can describe what you want, the more narrowly and effectively you can formulate the questions you ask to ensure that you get the right information.

Contextual inquiry refers to a whole set of methods that, collectively, form the most powerful and comprehensive toolkit for understanding your users in the context of their everyday lives (hence the name). These techniques are derived from the methods used by anthropologists to study cultures and societies. Applied on a smaller scale, the same methods used to examine, for example, how a nomadic tribe functions, can also be used to examine how people who buy aircraft parts function. The only downside is that contextual inquiry can be very time-consuming and very expensive. If you have the resources, and your problem requires a deep understanding of your users, a full-blown contextual inquiry study can reveal subtleties of user behavior that can't be discovered through other methods.

In other cases, contextual methods can be lightweight and inexpensive, although they tend not to produce the deep understanding of a full research study. One example of a method closely related to contextual inquiry is **task analysis**. The idea behind task analysis is that every user's interaction with a product takes place in the context of some task that user is performing. Sometimes the task is very focused (such as buying movie tickets) and sometimes it's broader (such as learning about international commerce regulations). Task analysis is a method of closely examining the precise steps users go through in accomplishing those tasks. This examination can be done either through interviews in which you get users to tell you stories about their experiences or through direct observation in the field, studying the users in their natural habitat.

User testing is the most commonly employed form of user research. User testing is not about testing your users; instead, it's about getting your users to test what you've produced. Sometimes user tests work with a finished product, either in preparation for a redesign or to root out any usability issues before launch. In other cases, users can test a work in progress or even a rough prototype of the finished product.

If you've done any reading about Web design at all, you've probably come across the concept of *usability*. This word means different things to different people. Some people use it to refer to the practice of testing designs with representative users. For others, it means adopting a very specific development methodology.

Every approach to usability seeks to make products easier to use. Many different definitions and lists of rules set out to codify what constitutes a usable Web site design. Some of them even agree with each other. But they all have the same principle at their core: Users need usable products. It's the most universal user need of all.

Tests with a fully operational Web site can be very broad or very narrow in scope. As with surveys or focus groups, it's best if you have a clear sense of what you want to investigate before you sit down with users. That doesn't mean, however, that a user test has to be strictly limited to assessing how successfully users complete a narrowly defined task. User testing can also investigate broader, less concrete issues. For example, a user test could be used to find out whether modifications to the design reinforce or undermine the company's brand message.

Another approach to user testing is to have users work with prototypes. These can take a variety of forms, from rough sketches on paper, to "lo-fi" mockups using stripped-down interface designs, to "click-through" prototypes that create the illusion of a finished product. Larger-scale projects employ different kinds of prototypes at different stages to gather user input all the way through the design process.

Sometimes user tests don't involve the site at all. You can recruit users to perform a variety of exercises that can give you insights into how they approach the subject matter of your site. For information-oriented sites, **card sorting** is one method used to explore how users categorize or group information elements. The user is given a stack of index cards, each of which has the name, description, or image of a piece or type of content on it. The user then sorts the cards into piles according to the groups or categories that feel most natural. Analyzing the results of card sorts conducted with several users can help us understand how they think about the information our site provides.

Creating Personas

Collecting all sorts of data about your users can be incredibly valuable, but sometimes you can lose sight of the real people behind all the statistics. You can make your users more real by turning them into **personas** (sometimes called user models or user profiles). A persona is a fictional character constructed to represent the needs of a whole range of real users. By putting a face and a name on the disconnected bits of data from your user research and segmentation work, personas can help ensure that you keep the users in mind during the design process.

INTERESTING CLAIM .

Let's look at an example. Suppose our site is designed to provide information for people who are starting their own businesses. We know from our research that our audience mostly falls in the 30–45 age range. Our users tend to be fairly comfortable with the Web and technology in general. Some of them have a lot of experience in the

business world; for others, this is their first exposure to all of the issues involved in running a business.

In this case, it might be appropriate to create two personas. We'll call the first one Janet. She's 42 years old, she's married, and she has two kids. She's spent the last couple of years as a vice president at a large accounting firm. She's become frustrated with working for other people, and now she wants to build a company of her own.

The second persona is Frank. He's 37 years old and married with one child. Woodworking has been a weekend hobby of Frank's for many years. Some friends of his were impressed by some furniture he made, so he's been thinking he could go into business for himself selling his work. He's not sure if he'll have to quit his job as a school bus driver in order to launch his new business.

Where did all this information come from? Well, for the most part, we made it up. We want our personas to be consistent with what we know about the users from our research, but the specific details of our personas are fictional inventions, used to breathe life into these characters who will stand in for our real, live users.

Janet and Frank represent the range of user needs we'll have to keep in mind as we're making decisions about the user experience of our site. To help us remember them and their needs, we'll grab a couple of stock photos to give Janet and Frank a little more identity, and combine those photos with the information about them we've put together. These profiles can be printed out and posted around the office so that when we have decisions to make we can ask ourselves (and each other): "Would that work for Janet? How would Frank react to it?" The personas help us keep our users in mind every step of the way.

Janet

"I don't have time to sort through a lot of information. I need quick answers."

Janet is frustrated with working in a corporate environment and wants to start her own accounting practice.

Age: 42
Occupation: Accounting firm vice president
Family: Married, two children
Household income: $180,000/year

Technical profile: Fairly comfortable with technology; Dell laptop (about one year old) running Windows; 5 Mbit Internet connection; 15-20 hours/week online
Internet use: 75% at home; news and information, shopping

Favorite sites:

WSJ.com   Salon.com   Travelocity.com

Personas are fictional characters drawn from user research who serve as example cases during user experience development.

Frank

"This stuff is all new to me. I want a site that will explain everything."

Frank is interested in learning how he can turn his hobby of making furniture into a business.

Age: 37
Occupation: School bus driver
Family: Married, one child
Household income: $60,000/year

Technical profile: Somewhat uncomfortable with technology; Apple iMac (about two years old); DSL Internet connection; 8-10 hours/week online
Internet use: 100% at home; entertainment, shopping

Favorite sites:

ESPN.com   moviefone.com   eBay.com

Team Roles and Process

Strategic issues affect everyone involved in the user experience design process. But despite this fact (or perhaps because of it), responsibility for formulating these objectives often falls through the cracks. Consulting firms will sometimes employ **strategists** on client projects to manage these issues—but because such rarefied expertise tends to be expensive, and because strategists aren't directly responsible for building any piece of the product itself, this line item is often one of the first to be cut from a project budget.

Strategists will talk to many people throughout the organization to get as many perspectives as possible on the questions of product objectives and user needs. **Stakeholders** are senior decision-makers who are responsible for parts of the organization that will be affected by the ultimate strategic direction of the product. For example, in the case of a Web site designed to provide customers with access to product support information, stakeholders might include representatives from marketing communications and customer service as well as product managers. It depends on the formal decision-making structure (and the informal political realities) of the organization.

One group often neglected in formulating a strategy is the rank and file—the people responsible for keeping the organization running on a day-to-day basis. But these people often have a better sense of what works and what doesn't than their managers do. They can inform the strategy in ways senior decision-makers can't—especially when it comes to user needs. No one knows what customers are having trouble with better than the people who talk to those customers every day. I am often surprised at how infrequently customer feedback finds its way to the product design and development teams who need it.

Product objectives and user needs are often defined in a formal **strategy document** or vision document. This document isn't just a list of objectives—it provides an analysis of the relationships among the various objectives and of how those objectives fit into the larger context of the organization. The objectives and their analysis are often supported by direct quotes from stakeholders, rank-and-file employees, and users themselves. These quotes vividly illustrate the strategic issues involved in the project. User needs are sometimes documented in a separate user research report (though there are certain advantages to having all your information in one place).

Bigger is not necessarily better when it comes to documenting your strategy. You don't have to include every data point and every supporting quote to get your idea across. Keep it concise and to the point. Remember that many people who will be exposed to the document won't have the time or interest to wade through hundreds of pages of supporting material, and it's far more important that they understand the strategy than that they be impressed by the volume of verbiage you've produced. An effective strategy document not only serves as a touchstone for the user experience development team; it can also be used to build support for the project in other parts of the organization.

The worst thing you can do with your strategy document is limit your team's access to it. The document wasn't created to be filed away somewhere or shared only with a handful of senior staff members—if the effort that went into it is going to pay off, the document has to be used actively during the project. All participants—designers, developers, project managers—need the strategy document to make informed decisions about their work. Strategy documents often contain sensitive material, but organizations can go too far and keep the strategy away from the responsible team, which undermines their ability to realize it.

Strategy should be the beginning of your user experience design process, but that doesn't mean your strategy must be set in stone before the project can move forward. Although trying to hit a moving target can be a tremendous waste of time and resources (not to mention a huge source of internal frustration), strategies can and should evolve and be refined. When revised and refined systematically, strategy work can be a continuing source of inspiration throughout the user experience design process.

chapter 4

The Scope Plane

Functional Specifications and
Content Requirements

With a clear sense of what we want and what our

users want, we can figure out how to satisfy all those

strategic objectives. Strategy becomes scope when

you translate user needs and product objectives into

specific requirements for what content and function-

ality the product will offer to users.

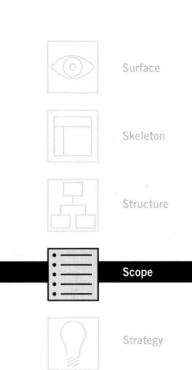

Surface

Skeleton

Structure

Scope

Strategy

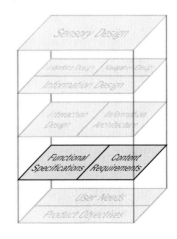

Defining the Scope

We do some things because there's value in the process, like jogging or practicing scales on the piano. We do other things because there's value in the product, like making a cheesecake or fixing a car. Defining the scope of your project is both: a valuable process that results in a valuable product.

The process is valuable because it forces you to address potential conflicts and rough spots in the product while the whole thing is still hypothetical. We can identify what we can tackle now and what will have to wait until later.

The product is valuable because it gives the entire team a reference point for all the work to be done throughout the project and a common language for talking about that work. Defining your requirements drives ambiguity out of the design process.

I once worked on a Web application that seemed to be in a state of perpetual beta: almost, but not quite, ready to roll out to actual users. A lot of things were wrong with our approach—the technology was shaky, we didn't seem to know anything about our users, and I was the only person in the whole company who had any experience at all with developing for the Web.

But none of this explains why we couldn't get the product to launch. The big stumbling block was an unwillingness to define requirements. After all, it was a lot of hassle to write everything down when we all worked in the same office anyway, and besides, the product manager needed to focus his energy on coming up with new features.

The result was a product that was an ever-changing mishmash of features in various stages of completeness. Every new article somebody read or every new thought that came along while somebody was playing with the product inspired another feature for consideration. There was a constant flow of work going on, but there was no schedule, there were no milestones, and there was no end in sight. Because no one knew the scope of the project, how could anyone know when we were finished?

There are two main reasons to bother to define requirements.

Reason #1: So You Know What You're Building

This seems kind of obvious, but it came as a surprise to the team building that Web application. If you clearly articulate exactly what you're setting out to build, everyone will know what the project's goals are and when they've been reached. The final product stops being an amorphous picture in the product manager's head, and it becomes something concrete that everyone at every level of the organization, from top executives to entry-level engineers, can work with.

In the absence of clear requirements, your project will probably turn out like a schoolyard game of "Telephone"—each person on the team gets an impression of the product via word of mouth, and everyone's description ends up slightly different. Or even worse, everyone assumes someone else is managing the design and development of some crucial aspect of the product, when in fact no one is.

Having a defined set of requirements allows you to parcel out responsibility for the work more efficiently. Seeing the entire scope mapped out enables you to see connections between individual requirements that might not otherwise be apparent. For example, in early discussions, the support documentation and the product spec sheets may have seemed like separate content features, but defining them as requirements might make it apparent that there's a lot of overlap and that the same group should be responsible for both.

Reason #2: So You Know What You're Not Building

Lots of features sound like good ideas, but they don't necessarily align with the strategic objectives of the project. Additionally, all sorts of possibilities for features emerge after the project is well underway. Having clearly identified requirements provides you with a framework for evaluating those ideas as they come along, helping you understand how (or if) they fit into what you've already committed to build.

Knowing what you're not building also means knowing what you're not building *right now*. The real value in collecting all those great ideas comes from finding appropriate ways to fit them into your long-term plans. By establishing concrete sets of requirements, and stockpiling requests that don't fit as possibilities for future releases, you can manage the entire process in a more deliberate way.

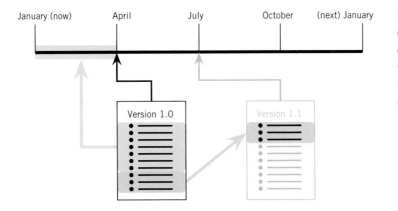

January (now)   April   July   October   (next) January

Version 1.0

Version 1.1

Requirements that can't be met in the current schedule can form the basis for the next milestone in your development cycle.

If you don't consciously manage your requirements, you'll get caught in the dreaded "scope creep." The image this always brings to mind for me is the snowball that rolls forward an inch—and then another—picking up a little extra snow with each turn until it is barreling down the hill, getting bigger and harder to stop all the way down. Likewise, each additional requirement may not seem like that much extra work. But put them all together, and you've got a project rolling away out of control, crushing deadlines and budget estimates on its way toward an inevitable final crash.

Functionality and Content

On the scope plane, we start from the abstract question of "Why are we making this product?" that we dealt with in the strategy plane and build upon it with a new question: "What are we going to make?"

The split between the Web as a vehicle for functionality and the Web as an information medium starts coming into play on the scope plane. On the functionality side, we're concerned with what would be considered the feature set of the software product. On the information side, we're dealing with content, the traditional domain of editorial and marketing communications groups.

Content and functionality seem just about as different as two things could be, but when it comes to defining scope, they can be addressed in very similar ways. Throughout this chapter, I'll use the term *feature* to refer to both software functions and content offerings.

In software development, the scope is defined through functional requirements or **functional specifications**. Some organizations use these terms to mean two different documents: requirements at the beginning of the project to describe what the system should do, and specifications at the end to describe what it actually does. In other cases, the specifications are developed soon after the requirements, filling in details of implementation. But most of the time, these terms are interchangeable—in fact, some people use the term *functional requirements specification* just to make sure they've covered all the bases. I'll use *functional specifications* to refer to the document itself, and *requirements* to refer to its contents.

The language of this chapter is mostly the language of software development. But the concepts here apply equally to content. Content development often involves a less formal requirements-definition process than software does, but the underlying principles are the same. A content developer will sit down and talk with people or pore over source material, whether that be a database or a drawer full of news clippings, in order to determine what information needs to be included in the content she's developing. This process for defining **content requirements** is actually not all that different from the technologist brainstorming features with stakeholders and reviewing existing documentation. The purposes and approaches are the same.

Content requirements often have functional implications. These days, pure content sites are usually handled through a **content management system (CMS)**. These systems come in all shapes and sizes, from very large and complex systems that dynamically generate pages from a dozen different data sources to lightweight tools optimized for managing one specific type of content feature in the most efficient way. You might decide to purchase a proprietary content management system, use one of the many open-source alternatives, or even build one from scratch. In any case, it will take some tinkering to tailor the system to your organization and your content.

A content management
system can automate
the workflow required
to produce and deliver
content to users.

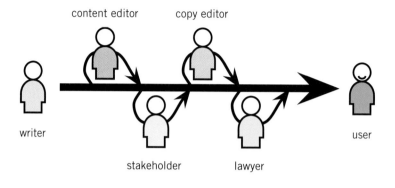

content editor   copy editor

writer

stakeholder   lawyer

user

The functionality you need in your content management system
will depend on the nature of the content you'll be managing. Will
you be maintaining content in multiple languages or data formats?
The CMS will need to be able to handle all those kinds of content
elements. Does every press release need to be approved by six executive vice presidents and a lawyer? The CMS will need to support
that kind of approval process in its workflow. Will content elements
be dynamically recombined according to the preferences of each
user, or the device they are using? The CMS will need to be able to
accomplish that level of complex delivery.

Similarly, the functional requirements of any technology product
have content implications. Will there be instructions on the preferences configuration screen? How about error messages? Somebody has to write those. Every time I see an error message on a
Web site like "Null input field exception," I know some engineer's
placeholder message made it into the final product because nobody
made that error message a content requirement. Countless allegedly
technical projects could have been improved immeasurably if the
developers had simply taken the time to have someone look at the
application with an eye toward content.

Defining Requirements

Some requirements apply to the product as a whole. Branding requirements are one common example of this; certain technical requirements, such as supported browsers and operating systems, are another.

Other requirements apply only to a specific feature. Most of the time when people refer to a requirement, they are thinking of a short description of a single feature the product is required to have.

The level of detail in your requirements will often depend on the specific scope of the project. If the goal of the project is to implement one very complex subsystem, a very high level of detail might be needed, even though the scope of the project relative to the larger site might be quite small. Conversely, a very large-scale content project might involve such a homogeneous base of content (such as a large number of functionally identical PDFs of product manuals) that the content requirements can only be very general.

The most productive source for requirements will always be your users themselves. But more often, your requirements will come from stakeholders, people in your organization who have some say over what goes into your product.

In either case, the best way to find out what people want is simply to ask them. The user research techniques outlined in Chapter 3 can all be used to help you get a better understanding of the kinds of features users want to see in your product.

Whether you are defining requirements with help from stakehold-ers inside your organization or working directly with users, the requirements that come out of the process will fall into three general categories. First, and most obvious, are the things people say they want. Some of these are very clearly good ideas and will find their way into the final product.

Sometimes the things people say they want are not the things they *actually* want. It's not uncommon for anyone, when they encounter some difficulty with a process or a product, to imagine a solution. Sometimes that solution is unworkable, or it addresses a symptom rather than the underlying cause of the problem. By exploring these suggestions, you can sometimes arrive at completely different requirements that solve the real problem.

The third type of requirement is the feature people don't know they want. When you get people talking about strategic objectives and new requirements that might fulfill them, sometimes they'll hit upon great ideas that simply hadn't occurred to anyone during the ongoing maintenance of the product. These often come out of brainstorming exercises, when participants have a chance to talk through and explore the possibilities for the project.

Ironically, sometimes the people most deeply involved in creating and working with a product are the ones least able to imagine new directions for it. When you spend all your time immersed in maintaining an existing product, you can often forget which of your constraints are real, and which are simply products of historical choices. For this reason, group brainstorming sessions that bring together people from diverse parts of the organization or represent diverse user groups can be very effective tools in opening the minds of participants to possibilities they wouldn't have considered before.

Getting an engineer, a customer service agent, and a marketing person in a room together to talk about the same Web site can be enlightening for everyone. Hearing unfamiliar perspectives—and having the opportunity to respond to them—encourages people to think in broader terms about both the problems involved in developing the product and the possible solutions.

Whatever device we are designing for—or if we are designing the device itself—our feature set will need to take into account hardware requirements, too. Does the device have a camera? GPS? Gyroscopic position sensors? These considerations will inform and constrain your functional possibilities.

Generating requirements is often a matter of finding ways to remove impediments. For example, assume that you have a user who has already decided to purchase a product—they just haven't decided if your product is the one they will buy. What can your site do to make this process—first selecting your product, and then buying your product—easier for them?

In Chapter 3, we looked at the technique of creating fictional characters called personas to help us better understand user needs. In determining requirements, we can use those personas again by putting our fictional characters into little stories called **scenarios**. A scenario is a short, simple narrative describing how a persona might go about trying to fulfill one of those user needs. By imagining the process our users might go through, we can come up with potential requirements to help meet their needs.

We can also look to our competitors for inspiration. Anyone else in the same business is almost certainly trying to meet the same user needs and is probably trying to accomplish similar product objectives as well. Has a competitor found a particularly effective feature to meet one of these strategic objectives? How have they addressed the same trade-offs and compromises we face?

Even products that aren't direct competitors can serve as fertile sources for possible requirements. Some gaming platforms, for example, offer users the ability to create social groups of fellow players. Adopting or building on their approach when scoping a similar feature for our digital video recorder may give us an advantage over our direct competition.

Functional Specifications

Functional specifications have something of a bad reputation in certain quarters. ~~Programmers often hate specs because they tend to be terribly dull, and the time spent reading them is time taken away from producing code.~~ As a result, specs go unread, which in turn reinforces the impression that producing them is a waste of time—because it is! A bad approach to specs becomes a self-fulfilling prophecy.

One complaint about functional specifications is that they don't reflect the actual product. Things change during implementation. Everybody understands this—it's the nature of working with technology. Sometimes something you thought would work didn't, or more likely didn't quite work the way you thought it would. This, however, is not a reason to abandon writing specs as a lost cause. Instead, it highlights the importance of specs that actually work. When things change during implementation, the answer is not to throw up your hands and declare the futility of writing specs. The answer is to make the process of defining specifications lightweight enough that the spec doesn't become a project separate from developing the product itself.

In other words, ~~documentation won't solve your problems. Defini-~~ ~~tion will. It's not about volume or detail. It's~~ about clarity and accu-racy. ~~Specs don't have to embody every aspect of the product—just~~ ~~the ones that need definition to avoid confusion in the design~~ and ~~development process.~~ And specs don't need to capture some ideal-ized future state for the product—just the decisions that have been made in the course of creating it.

Writing It Down

No matter how large or complex the project may be, a few general rules apply to writing any kind of requirements.

Be positive. Instead of describing a bad thing the system shouldn't do, describe what it will do to prevent that bad thing. For example, instead of this:

> *The system will not allow the user to purchase a kite without*
> *kite string.*

This would be better:

> *The system will direct the user to the kite string page if the user tries*
> *to buy a kite without string.*

Be specific. Leaving as little as possible open to interpretation is the only way we can determine whether a requirement has been fulfilled.

Compare these examples:

1. *The most popular videos will be highlighted.*
2. *Videos with the most views in the last week will appear at the*
   top of the list.

The first example seems to identify a clear requirement, but it does not take much investigation to start poking holes in it. What counts as popular? Videos with the most comments? The ones with the most "like" votes? And what constitutes highlighting them?

The second example defines our goal in specific detail, defining what we mean by popular and describing a mechanism for highlighting. By removing the possibility of differing interpretations, the second requirement neatly skirts the kinds of arguments likely to crop up during or after implementation.

Avoid subjective language. This is really just another way of being specific and removing ambiguity—and therefore the possibility for misinterpretation—from the requirements.

Here's a highly subjective requirement:

> *The site will have a hip, flashy style.*

Requirements must be falsifiable—that is, it must be possible to demonstrate when a requirement has not been met. It's difficult to demonstrate whether subjective qualities like hip and flashy have been fulfilled. My idea of hipness probably doesn't match yours, and most likely the CEO has another idea entirely.

This doesn't mean you can't require that your site be hip. You just have to find ways to specify which criteria will be applied:

> *The site will meet the hipness expectations of Wayne, the mail clerk.*

Wayne normally wouldn't have any say about the project, but our project sponsor clearly respects his sense of hipness. Hopefully it's the same sense our users have. But the requirement is still rather

arbitrary because we're relying on Wayne's approval instead of criteria that can be more objectively defined. So perhaps this requirement would be best of all:

> *The look of the site will conform to the company branding guidelines*
> *document.*

The whole concept of hipness has now disappeared entirely from
the requirement. Instead, we have a clear, unambiguous reference
to established guidelines. To make sure the branding guidelines are
sufficiently hip, the VP of marketing may consult Wayne the mail
clerk, or she may consult her teenage daughter, or she may even
consult some user research findings. It's up to her. But now we can
say definitively whether the requirement has been met.

We can also eliminate subjectivity by defining some requirements
quantitatively. Just as success metrics make strategic goals quan-
tifiable, defining a requirement in quantitative terms can help us
identify whether we've met the requirement. For example, instead
of requiring that the system have "a high level of performance," we
can require that the system be designed to support at least 1,000
simultaneous users. If the final product only allows three-digit user
numbers, we can tell the requirement hasn't been met.

Content Requirements

Much of the time, when we talk about content, we're referring to
text. But images, audio, and video can be more important than the
accompanying text. These different content types can also work
together to fulfill a single requirement. For example, a content

feature covering a sporting event might have an article accompanied by photographs and video clips. Identifying all the content types associated with a feature can help you determine what resources will be needed to produce the content (or whether it can be produced at all).

Don't get confused between the *format* of a piece of content and its *purpose*. When discussing content requirements with stakeholders, one of the first things I usually hear is, "We should have FAQs." But the term *FAQ* really only refers to a content format: a simple series of questions and answers. The real value of an FAQ to users is that it provides ready access to commonly needed information. Other content requirements can fulfill that same purpose; but when the focus is on the format, the purpose itself can be forgotten. More often than not, FAQs neglect the "frequently" part of the equation, offering instead answers to whatever questions the content provider could think of to satisfy the FAQ requirement.

The expected size of each of your content features has a huge influence on the user experience decisions you will have to make. Your content requirements should provide rough estimates of the size of each feature: word count for text features, pixel dimensions for images or video, and file sizes for downloadable, stand-alone content elements like audio files or PDF documents. These size estimates don't have to be precise—approximations are fine. We only have to collect the essential information needed to design an appropriate vehicle for that content. Designing a site to provide access to small thumbnail images is different from designing a site to provide access to full-screen photographs; knowing in advance the size of the content elements we have to accommodate enables us to make smart, informed decisions along the way.

It's important to identify who will be responsible for each content element as early as possible. Once it has been validated against our strategic objectives, any content feature inevitably sounds like a really good idea—as long as someone else is responsible for creating and maintaining it. If we get too deep into the development process without identifying who will be responsible for every required content feature, we're likely to end up with gaping holes in our site because those features everybody loved when they were hypothetical turned out to be too much work for anyone to actually take on.

And that's what people often forget when developing requirements: Content is hard work. You might be able to hire on contract resources (or, more likely, stick someone down in marketing with the job) to create the content in time for the initial launch, but who will keep it up to date? Content—well, effective content, anyway—requires constant maintenance. Approaching content as if you can post it and forget it leads to a site that, over time, does an increasingly poor job of meeting user needs.

This is why, for every content feature, you should identify how frequently it will be updated. The frequency of updates should be derived from your strategic goals for the site: Based on your product objectives, how often do you want users to come back? Based on the needs of your users, how often do they expect updated information? However, keep in mind that the ideal frequency of updates for your users ("I want to know everything instantly, 24 hours a day!") may not be practical for your organization. You'll have to arrive at a frequency that represents a reasonable compromise between the expectations of your users and your available resources.

If your site has to serve multiple audiences with divergent needs, knowing which audience a piece of content is intended for can help you make better decisions about how to present that content. Information intended for children requires a different approach from information intended for their parents; information for both of them needs yet a third approach.

For projects that involve working with a lot of existing content, much of the information that will feed your requirements is recorded in a **content inventory**. Taking an inventory of all the content on your existing site may seem like a tedious process—and it usually is. But having the inventory (which usually takes the form of a simple, albeit very large, spreadsheet) is important for the same reason that having concrete requirements is important: so everyone on the team knows exactly what they have to work with in creating the user experience.

Prioritizing Requirements

Collecting ideas for possible requirements is not hard. Almost everyone who regularly comes in contact with a product—whether they are inside the organization or outside—will have at least one idea for a feature that could be added. The tricky part is sorting out what features should be included in the scope for your project.

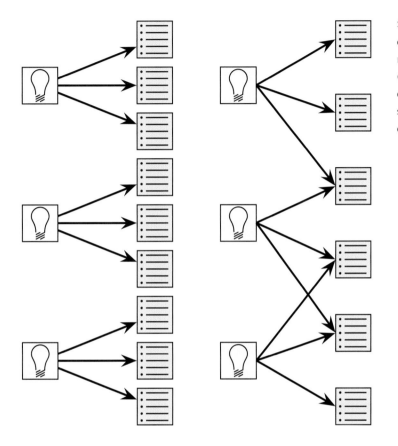

Sometimes a strategic objective will result in multiple requirements (left). In other cases, one requirement can serve multiple strategic objectives (right).

It's actually fairly rare that you see a simple one-to-one correlation between your strategic objectives and your requirements. Sometimes one requirement can be applied toward multiple strategic objectives. Similarly, one objective will often be associated with several different requirements.

Because the scope is built upon the strategy, we'll need to evaluate possible requirements based on whether they fulfill our strategic goals (both product objectives and user needs). In addition to those two considerations, defining the scope adds a third: How feasible will it be to actually make this stuff?

Some features can't be implemented because they're technically impossible—for example, there's just no way to allow users to smell products over the Web yet, no matter how badly they might want that ability. Other features (particularly in the case of content) aren't feasible because they would demand more resources—human or financial—than we have at our disposal. In other cases, it's just a matter of time: The feature would take three months to implement, but we have an executive requirement to launch in two.

In the case of time constraints, you can push features out to a later release or project milestone. For resource constraints, technological or organizational changes can sometimes—but, importantly, not always—reduce the resource burden, enabling a feature to be implemented. (However, impossible things will remain impossible. Sorry.)

Few features exist in a vacuum. Even content features on a Web site rely on the features around them to inform the user on how best to use the content provided. This inevitably leads to conflicts between features. Some features will require trade-offs with others in order to produce a coherent, consistent whole. For example, users may want a one-step order submission process—but the tangle of legacy databases the site uses can't accommodate all the data at once. Is it preferable to go with a multiple-step process, or should you rework the database system? It depends on your strategic objectives.

Keep an eye out for feature suggestions that indicate possible shifts in strategy that weren't apparent during the development of the vision document. Any feature suggestion not in line with the project strategy is, by definition, out of scope. But if a suggested feature that falls outside the scope doesn't fit any of the types of constraints above and still sounds like a good idea, you may want to reexamine some of your strategic objectives. If you find yourself revisiting many aspects of your strategy, however, you've probably jumped into defining requirements too soon.

If your strategy or vision document identifies a clear hierarchy of priorities among your strategic objectives, these priorities should be the primary factors in determining the priority of suggested features. Sometimes, however, the relative importance of two different strategic objectives isn't clear. In these cases, whether features end up in the project scope all too often comes down to corporate politics.

When stakeholders talk about strategy, they usually start out with feature ideas, and then have to be coaxed back to the underlying strategic factors. Because stakeholders often have trouble separating features from strategy, certain features will often have champions. Thus the requirements definition process becomes a matter of negotiation between motivated stakeholders.

Managing this negotiation process can be difficult. The best approach to resolving a conflict between stakeholders is to appeal to the defined strategy. Focus on strategic goals, not proposed means of accomplishing them. If you can assure a stakeholder with her heart set on a particular feature that the strategic goal the feature is intended to fulfill can be addressed in some other way, she won't feel the needs of her constituents are being neglected. Admittedly, this is often easier said than done. Demonstrating empathy with the needs of stakeholders is essential to resolving feature conflicts. Who says tech workers don't need people skills?

chapter 5

The Structure Plane

Interaction Design and Information Architecture

After the requirements have been defined and

prioritized, we have a clear picture of what will be

included in the final product. The requirements,

however, don't describe how the pieces fit together

to form a cohesive whole. This is the next level up

from scope: developing a conceptual structure for

the site.

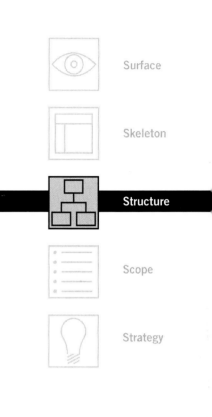

Surface

Skeleton

Structure

Scope

Strategy

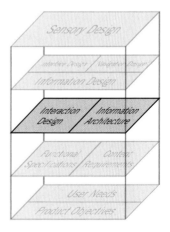

Defining the Structure

The realm of structure is the third of the five planes, and appropriately it is the point at which our concerns shift from the more abstract issues of strategy and scope to the concrete factors that will determine what users finally experience. But the line between abstract and concrete can be blurry—although much of what we decide here will have a noticeable, tangible influence on the final product, the decisions themselves still involve largely conceptual matters.

product as functionality | **product as information**

structure

Interaction Design / *Information Architecture*

skeleton

scope

In traditional software development, the discipline involved in creating a structured experience for the user is known as **interaction design**. It used to be lumped under the heading of "interface design," but interaction design is now recognized as a separate discipline.

In content development, structuring the user experience is a question of **information architecture**. This field draws on a number of disciplines that historically have been concerned with the organization, grouping, ordering, and presentation of content: library science, journalism, and technical communication, among others.

Interaction design and information architecture share an emphasis on defining patterns and sequences in which options will be presented to users. Interaction design concerns the options involved in performing and completing tasks. Information architecture deals with the options involved in conveying information to a user.

Interaction design and information architecture sound like esoteric, highly technical areas, but these disciplines aren't really about technology at all. They're about understanding people—the way they behave and think. By building this understanding into the structure of our product, we help ensure a successful experience for those who use it.

Interaction Design

Interaction design is concerned with describing possible user behavior and defining how the system will accommodate and respond to that behavior. Any time a person uses a product, a sort of dance goes on between the two of them. The user moves around, and the system responds. Then the user moves in response to the system, and so the dance goes on. But the typical way that software has been designed doesn't really acknowledge this dance. The thinking seems to have been that if every application danced a little bit differently anyway, it wasn't unreasonable to expect the user to adapt. The system could just do its thing, and if some toes got stepped on, well, that was part of the learning process. But every dancer will tell you that for the dance to really work, each participant must anticipate the moves of the other.

Programmers have traditionally focused on and cared most about two aspects of software: what it does and how it does it. There's a good reason for this—it is precisely their passion for these details that makes programmers good at what they do. But this focus meant that programmers would gravitate toward building a system in the way that was most technically efficient without regard to what worked best for users. Especially back when computing power was a limited resource, the best approach was the one that got the job done within those technical limitations.

The approach that works best for the technology is almost never the approach that works best for the person using it. Thus, software acquired the reputation that has haunted it for most of its existence: Software is complicated, confusing, and hard to use. This is why, for years, "computer literacy"—teaching people about the inner workings of computers—was widely considered to be the only way to make users and software get along.

It took a long time, but as we learned more about how people used technology, eventually we started catching on to the idea that, instead of designing software that works best for the machine, we could design software that works best for the people who use it, thereby skipping this whole business of sending file clerks to programming classes to improve their computer literacy. The new discipline that arose to help software developers do this is called interaction design.

Conceptual Models

Users' impressions of how the interactive components we create will behave are known as **conceptual models**. For example, does the system treat a particular feature as a thing the user consumes, a place the user visits, or an object the user acquires? Different sites take different approaches. Knowing your conceptual model allows you to make consistent design decisions. It doesn't matter whether the content element is a place or an object; what matters is that the site behaves consistently, instead of treating the element as a place sometimes and an object at other times.

For example, the conceptual model for the shopping cart component of a typical e-commerce site is that of a container. This metaphorical concept influences both the design of the component and the language we use in the interface. A container holds objects; as a result, we "put things into" and "take things out of" the "cart," and the system must provide functions to accomplish these tasks.

Suppose the conceptual model for the component were a different real-world analog, such as a catalog order form. The system might provide an edit function that would replace both the add and remove functions of the traditional cart, and instead of using a checkout metaphor to complete the process, users might send their orders in.

Both the retail store model and the catalog model seem perfectly suitable for allowing users to place orders over the Web. Which to choose? The retail store model is so widely used on the Web that it's taken on the status of a **convention**. If your users do a lot of shopping on other Web sites, you'll probably want to stick to that convention. Using conceptual models people are already familiar with makes it easier for them to adapt to an unfamiliar site. Of course, there's nothing wrong with breaking away from convention either—as long as you have a good reason for doing so and have an alternate conceptual model that will meet your users' needs while still making sense to them. Unfamiliar conceptual models are only effective when users can correctly understand and interpret them.

A conceptual model can refer to just one component of a system or to the system as a whole. When the news and commentary site Slate launched, its conceptual model was a real-world magazine: The site had a front and a back, and every page had both a page number and interface elements allowing the user to "turn the page." As it turns out, the magazine conceptual model doesn't translate very effectively to the Web, and Slate eventually dropped it.

We don't have to communicate our conceptual models to our users explicitly—in fact, sometimes this only confuses users instead of helping them. It's more important that conceptual models are used consistently throughout the development of the interaction design. Understanding the models users themselves bring to the site (Does it work like a retail store? Does it work like a catalog?) helps us choose the conceptual models that will work most effec-tively. Ideally, the users won't have to be told what conceptual model we're following; they'll pick up on it intuitively as they use the site because the behavior of the site will match their implicit expectations.

Basing our conceptual models on metaphors involving real-world analogs to system functions can be valuable, but it's important not to take our metaphors too literally. The home page of the site for Southwest Airlines used to consist solely of a picture of a customer service desk, with a stack of brochures to one side, a telephone to the other side, and so on. For years, the site was held up as an example of a conceptual model gone too far—placing a reservation may be analogous to making a phone call, but that doesn't mean the reservation system should actually be represented by a telephone. Southwest must have gotten tired of being used as a bad example; its site subsequently became light on metaphor and considerably more functional.

The old Southwest Airlines site is a classic example of conceptual models being tied too closely to real-world counterparts.

Error Handling

A huge part of any interaction design project involves dealing with user error—what does the system do when people make mistakes, and what can the system do to prevent those mistakes from happening in the first place?

The first and best defense against errors is to design the system so that errors are simply impossible. A good example of this type of defense can be seen in any car with an automatic transmission. Starting the car while the transmission is engaged can damage the sensitive and complex transmission mechanism; moreover, the car doesn't actually start, but instead lurches forward abruptly. Bad for the car, bad for the driver, and possibly bad for an innocent bystander who happens to be in the path of the lurching car.

To prevent this, any car with an automatic transmission is designed so the starter won't engage unless the transmission is disengaged. Because it's impossible to start the car with the transmission engaged, the error never happens. Unfortunately, it's not quite so easy to make most user errors impossible in this way.

The next best thing to making errors impossible is to make them merely difficult. But even with such measures in place, some errors are bound to happen. At this point, the system should do what it can to help the user figure out the error and fix it. In some cases, the system can even fix the error on the user's behalf. But be careful— some of the most irritating behavior of software products results from well-intentioned efforts to correct user errors. (If you've ever used Microsoft Word, you know exactly what I'm talking about.

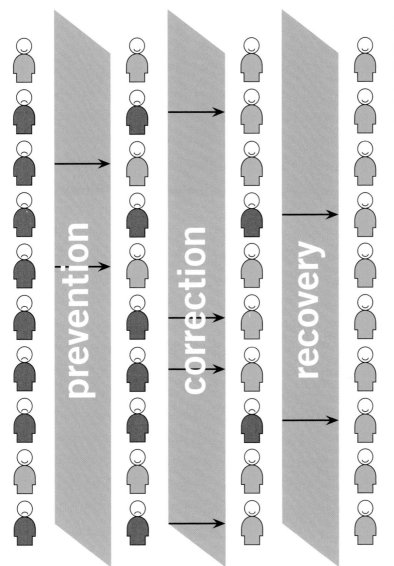

Each layer of error handling in your interaction design ensures that a higher percentage of users will have positive experiences.

Word offers numerous features intended to correct common errors; invariably, I find myself switching them off so I can stop correcting the corrections and get some work done.)

Helpful error messages and easy-to-interpret interfaces can help users catch many kinds of errors after they've happened. But some user actions may not appear to be errors until it's too late for the system to catch them. In these cases, the system should provide a way for users to recover from the error. The best-known example of this is the famous undo function, but error recovery can take many different forms. For errors that can't be recovered from, providing plenty of warning is the only means of prevention the system can provide. Of course, this warning is only effective when users actually notice it. Including too many "Are you sure?" confirmations can cause the really important ones to be overlooked—and often annoys more users than it helps.

Information Architecture

Information architecture is a new idea, but it's an old practice—in fact, you could say it's as old as human communication itself. For as long as people have had information to convey, they have had to make choices about how they structure that information so other people can understand and use it.

Because information architecture is concerned with how people cognitively process information, information architecture considerations come up in any product that requires users to make sense of the information presented. Obviously, these considerations are critical in the case of information-oriented products (like corporate information sites) but they can have a huge impact even in more functionality-oriented products (like a mobile phone).

Structuring Content

On content sites, information architecture is concerned with creating organizational and navigational schemes that allow users to move through site content efficiently and effectively. Information architecture on the Web is closely related to the field of information retrieval: the design of systems that enable users to find information easily. But Web site architectures are often called on to do more than just help people find things; in many cases, they have to educate, inform, or persuade users.

Most commonly, information architecture problems require creating categorization schemes that will correspond to our own objectives for the site, the user needs we intend to meet, and the content that will be incorporated in the site. We can tackle creating such a categorization scheme in two ways: from the top down, or from the bottom up.

A **top-down approach** to information architecture involves creating the architecture directly from an understanding of strategy plane considerations: product objectives and user needs. Starting with the broadest categories of possible content and functionality needed to accomplish these strategic goals, we then break the categories down into logical subsections. This hierarchy of categories and subcategories serves as the empty shell into which the content and functionality will be slotted.

A **bottom-up approach** to information architecture also derives categories and subcategories, but it does so based on an analysis of the content and functional requirements. Starting with the source material that exists (or that will exist by the time the site launches), we group items together into low-level categories and then group those into higher-level categories, building toward a structure that reflects our product objectives and user needs.

A top-down architectural approach is driven by considerations from the strategy plane.

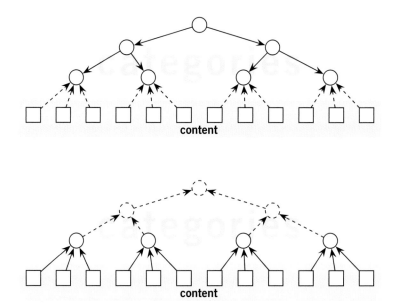

A bottom-up architectural approach is driven by considerations from the scope plane.

Neither approach is better than the other. Approaching the architecture from the top down can sometimes cause important details about the content itself to be overlooked. On the other hand, a bottom-up approach can sometimes result in an architecture so precisely tuned and fitted to the existing content that it isn't flexible enough to accommodate changes or additions. Striking a balance between top-down and bottom-up thinking is the only way to make sure the final result can avoid these pitfalls.

It's not necessary to adhere to a particular number of categories at any level or in any section of the architecture. The categories just have to be the right ones for your users and their needs. Some people favor counting the number of steps it takes to complete a task or the number of clicks it takes for a user to reach a particular destination as a way to evaluate the quality of a site structure. The most important sign of quality, however, is not how many steps the process took, but whether each step made sense to the user and whether it followed naturally from the previous step. Users will invariably favor a clearly defined seven-step process over a confusingly compressed three-step alternative.

Web sites are living entities. They require constant care and feeding. Inevitably, they grow and change over time. In most cases, a few new requirements acquired along the way shouldn't require rethinking the overall structure of the site. One trait of an effective structure is its ability to accommodate growth and adapt to change. But the accumulation of new content will eventually require a re-examination of the organizing principles employed on the site. For example, the architecture that enabled users to page through press releases day-by-day might have been fine when you had only a few months' worth, but organizing them by topic might be more practical after a few years.

The entire user experience, including the structure of the site, is built on an understanding of your objectives and the needs of your users. If what you want to accomplish with the site is redefined or the needs you intend the site to meet change, be prepared to rework the structure of your site accordingly. The need for such structural change rarely announces itself in advance, though; often, by the time you can tell that you need to rework the architecture, your users are already suffering.

An adaptable
architecture can
accommodate the
addition of new content
within a section (top)
as well as entire new
sections (bottom).

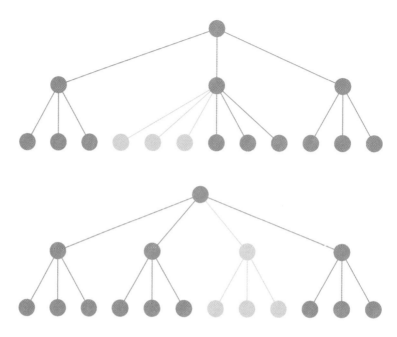

Architectural Approaches

The basic unit of information structures is the **node**. A node can correspond to any piece or group of information—it can be as small as a single number (like the price of a product) or as large as an entire library. By dealing with nodes rather than with pages, documents, or components, we can apply a common language and a common set of structural concepts to a diverse range of problems.

The abstraction of nodes also allows us to explicitly set the level of detail we will be concerned with. Most Web site architecture projects are only concerned with the arrangement of pages on the site; by identifying the page as our base-level node, we make it explicit that we won't be dealing with anything smaller. If the page itself is too small for the project at hand, we can have each node correspond to an entire section of the site. If the page is too big, we can define nodes as individual content elements within the page, and the page as a group of nodes.

These nodes can be arranged in many different ways, but these structures really fall into just a few general classes.

In a **hierarchical** structure—sometimes called a *tree* or *hub-and-spoke* structure—nodes have parent/child relationships with other related nodes. Child nodes represent narrower concepts within the broader category represented by the parent node. Not every node has children, but every node has a parent, leading all the way up to the parent node of the entire structure (or the root of the tree, if you prefer). Because the concept of hierarchical relationships is well understood by users and because software tends to work in hierarchies anyway, this type of structure is far and away the most common.

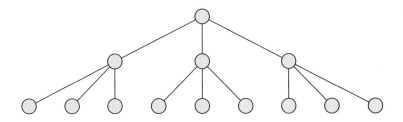

Hierarchical structure.

A **matrix** structure allows the user to move from node to node along two or more dimensions. Matrix structures are often useful for enabling users with different needs to navigate through the same content, because each user need can be associated with one axis of the matrix. For example, if some of your users really want to browse products by color, but others need to browse by size, a matrix can accommodate both groups. A matrix of more than three dimensions can cause problems, however, if you expect users to rely on it as their primary navigational tool. The human brain simply isn't very well equipped to visualize movement in four or more dimensions.

Matrix structure.

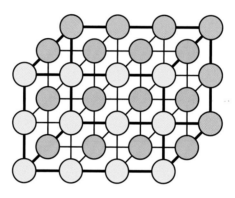

Organic structures don't attempt to follow any consistent pattern. Nodes are connected together on a case-by-case basis, and the architecture has no strong concept of sections. Organic structures are good for exploring a set of topics whose relationship is unclear or evolving. But organic structures don't provide users with a strong sense of where they are in the architecture. If you want to encourage a feeling of free-form exploration, such as on some entertainment or educational sites, an organic structure can be a good choice; however, it can present a challenge if your users need to reliably find their way back to the same piece of content again.

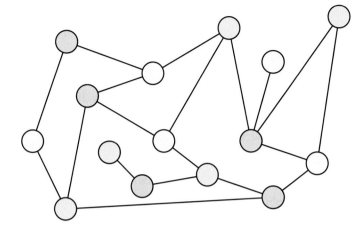

Organic structure.

Sequential structures are the ones you are most familiar with from offline media—in fact, you're experiencing one right now. The sequential flow of language is the most basic type of information architecture there is, and the faculties needed to process it are built right into our brains. Books, articles, audio, and video are all designed to be experienced in a sequential fashion. Sequential structures on the Web are used most often for smaller-scale structures such as individual articles or sections; large-scale sequential structures tend to be limited to applications in which the order of content presentation is essential to meeting user needs, such as in instructional material.

Sequential structure.

Organizing Principles

Nodes in an information structure are arranged according to **organizing principles**. At its most basic level, the organizing principle is the criterion by which we determine which nodes are grouped together and which are kept separate. Different organizing principles will be applied in different areas and at different levels of the site.

For example, in the case of a corporate information site, we might have categories near the top of our tree such as "Consumer," "Business," and "Investor." At this level, the organizing principle is the audience for which the content is intended. Another site might have top-level categories like "North America," "Europe," and "Africa." Using geography as an organizing principle is one approach to meeting the needs of a global audience.

Generally, the organizing principles you employ at the highest levels of your site are closely tied to the product objectives and user needs. At lower levels in the architecture, issues specific to the content and functional requirements begin to have a greater influence on the organizing principles that should be used.

For example, a site with news-oriented content will often have chronology as its most prominent organizing principle. Timeliness is the single most important factor for users (who, after all, look to news sites for information on current events, not history) as well as for the creators of the site (who must emphasize the timeliness of their content in order to remain competitive).

At the next level in the architecture, other factors more closely tied to content come into play. For a sports news site, the content might be divided into categories such as "Baseball," "Tennis," and "Hockey"; a more general-interest site might have categories like "International News," "National News," and "Local News."

Any collection of information—whether it consists of two items, 200, or 2,000—has an inherent conceptual structure. In fact, it usually has more than one. That's part of the problem we have to solve. The challenge isn't creating a structure, but creating the right structure for our objectives and the needs of our users.

For example, suppose our site contained a repository of information about cars. One possible organizing principle would arrange the information according to the weight of the car in question. So the first thing the user would see would be information about the heaviest car in our database, then the second heaviest, and on down to the lightest.

For a consumer information site, this is probably the wrong way to organize the information. Most people, most of the time, aren't concerned with the weight of a car. Organizing the information according to make, model, or type of car would probably be more appropriate for this audience. On the other hand, if our users are professionals who deal on a daily basis with the business of shipping cars overseas, weight becomes a very important factor. For these people, qualities like fuel economy and engine type are considerably less important, if they matter at all.

These attributes, in the language of library science, are known as facets, and they can provide a simple, flexible set of organizing principles for almost any content. But as the preceding example shows, using the wrong facets can be worse than using no facets at all. One common response to this problem is to position every conceivable facet as an organizing principle and let the users pick the one that's important to them.

Unfortunately, unless you're dealing with very simple information consisting of only a few facets, this approach soon turns the architecture into an unwieldy mess. The users have so many options to sort through that no one can find anything. The burden shouldn't be on the user to sort through all the attributes and pick out what's important—the burden is on us. The strategy tells us what the users need, and the scope tells us what information will meet those needs. In creating the structure, we identify the specific aspects of that information that will be foremost in the users' minds. A successful user experience is one in which the user's expectations are anticipated and accounted for.

Language and Metadata

Even if the structure is a perfectly accurate representation of the way people think about your subject matter, your users won't be able to find their way around the architecture if they can't understand your **nomenclature**: the descriptions, labels, and other terminology the site uses. For this reason, it's essential to use the language of your users and to do so in a consistent fashion. The tool we use to enforce that consistency is called a **controlled vocabulary**.

A controlled vocabulary is nothing more than a set of standard terms for use on the site. This is another area in which user research is essential. Talking to users and understanding how they communicate is the most effective way to develop a system of nomenclature that will feel natural to them. Creating and adhering to a controlled vocabulary that reflects the language of your users is the best way to prevent your organization's internal jargon from creeping onto the site, where it will only confuse your users.

Controlled vocabularies also help create consistency across all your content. Whether the people responsible for producing the content sit right next to each other or in offices on separate continents, the controlled vocabulary provides a definitive resource to ensure that everyone is speaking the user's language.

A more sophisticated approach to controlling vocabulary is to create a **thesaurus**. Unlike a simple list of approved terms, a thesaurus will also document alternative terms that are commonly used but not approved for use on the site. With a thesaurus, you can map internal jargon, shorthand, slang terms, or acronyms to their approved counterparts. A thesaurus might also include other types of relationships among the terms, providing recommendations for broader, narrower, or related terms. Documenting these relationships can give you a more complete picture of the entire range of concepts found in your content, which in turn can suggest additional architectural approaches.

Having a controlled vocabulary or thesaurus can be especially helpful if you decide to build a system that includes **metadata**. The term *metadata* means simply "information about information." It refers to a structured approach to describing a given piece of content.

Suppose we were dealing with an article about how your latest product is being used by volunteer fire departments. Some of the metadata for that article might include

- The name of the author
- The date the piece was posted
- The type of piece (for example, a case study or article)
- The name of the product
- The type of product
- The customer's industry (for example, volunteer fire department)
- Related topics (for example, municipal agencies or emergency services)

Having this information allows us to consider a range of possible architectural approaches that would be difficult (if not downright impossible) to implement without it. In short, ~~the more detailed information you have about your content, the more~~ flexibility ~~you have in structuring it~~. If emergency services suddenly shows potential as a lucrative new market for the company to expand into, having this metadata will allow us to rapidly create a new section to meet the needs of these users with the content we already have.

But creating technical systems to collect and track all this metadata won't help us if the data itself isn't consistent. That's where controlled vocabularies come in. By using only one term for each unique concept in your content, you can rely on automation to help define the connections between your content elements. Your site could dynamically link together all the pages on a specific topic without anyone having to do anything more than use the same term consistently in their metadata.

In addition, good metadata can provide a faster and more reliable way for your users to find information on your site than a basic full-text search engine can provide. Search engines can be powerful, but in general they're very, very dumb—you give them a string of characters, and they pretty much go looking for exactly that string of characters. They don't understand what any of it means.

Connecting your search engine with a thesaurus and providing metadata for your content can help make the engine smarter. The search engine can use the thesaurus to map a search for a disallowed term to a preferred term; then it can check the metadata for that preferred term. Instead of getting no results at all, the user gets highly targeted, relevant results—and maybe even some recommendations for other related subjects that might be of interest.

Team Roles and Process

The documents needed to describe the structure of a site—from the specific details of nomenclature and metadata to the big picture of overall information architecture and interaction design—can vary substantially depending on the complexity of the project. For projects involving a lot of content in a hierarchical structure, simple text outlines can be an effective way to document the architecture. In some cases, tools like spreadsheets and databases will be pressed into service to help capture the nuances of a complex architecture.

But the major documentation tool for information architecture or interaction design is the diagram. Representing the structure visually is the most efficient way for us to communicate the branches, groups, and interrelationships among the components of our site.

Web site structures are inherently complicated things; trying to convey this complexity in words pretty much guarantees that no one will read them.

In the early days of the Web, this kind of diagram was called a site map; but because *site map* is also a term used for a particular kind of navigational tool on a site (which you'll read more about in Chapter 6), *architecture diagram* is now the favored term for the tool we use internally to describe site structure.

The diagram doesn't have to document every link on every page in your site. In fact, in most cases that level of detail only serves to confuse and obscure the information the team really needs. It's more important to document conceptual relationships: Which categories go together, and which remain separate? How do the steps in a given interaction sequence fit together?

Early in my career, I found myself having to express the same basic interaction structures over and over again from project to project. Over time, I started standardizing the way I illustrated my ideas in my site diagrams. I settled on a particular set of shapes that I used, and defined what each of those shapes meant.

The system I created to diagram site structures is called the Visual Vocabulary. Since I first posted it to the Web in 2000, information architects and interaction designers all over the world have adopted it. You can learn more about the Visual Vocabulary, see sample diagrams, and download tools for using it at my Web site: www.jjg.net/ia/visvocab/.

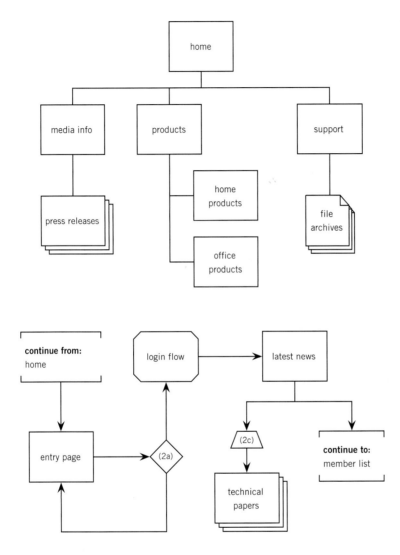

The Visual Vocabulary is a system for diagramming architectures ranging from the very simple (top) to the very complex (bottom). See www.jjg.net/ia/visvocab/ for more details.

Many organizations employ full-time user experience designers who bear responsibility for structural issues. In other organizations, however, responsibility for structure often lands in someone's lap by default rather than through conscious planning. Who ends up responsible for structure often depends on the culture of the organization or the nature of the project.

For content-heavy sites or in organizations in which creating a presence on the Web was initially seen as a marketing activity, the responsibility for determining the structure of the site has resided within content development, editorial, or marketing communications groups. If the organization has historically been led by technical people or had a technology-oriented internal culture, responsibility for structure has commonly fallen to the technical project manager working on the Web site.

Every project can benefit from having a full-time specialist dedicated to structural issues. Sometimes this person goes by the job title interaction designer, but others prefer to be referred to as an information architect. Don't let the title confuse you—although it's true that some information architects specialize exclusively in creating organizational schemes and navigational structures for content sites, more often than not, an information architect will have some degree of experience with interaction design issues and vice versa. Because information architecture and interaction design issues are often so closely related, user experience designer has become a more common title for someone with these skills.

Your organization might not have the volume of ongoing work to warrant hiring a full-time user experience designer as a permanent member of your staff. If your Web development efforts are mostly limited to keeping the content you have up-to-date and you don't do much new development between site-wide redesign projects every couple of years, a staff user experience designer probably isn't a good way to spend your money. But if you have a steady stream of new content and functionality being added to your site, a user experience designer can help you manage that process in the way that will be most effective for meeting the needs of your users and for meeting your own strategic objectives.

Whether you have a specialist to address structural concerns isn't important, but it is important that those concerns are addressed by *someone*. Your site will have a structure whether or not you plan it out. The sites that are built according to a clear structural plan tend to be the ones that require less frequent overhauls, produce concrete results for their owners, and satisfy the needs of their users.

chapter **6**

The Skeleton Plane

Interface Design, Navigation Design, and Information Design

The conceptual structure begins to give shape to the mass of requirements arising from our strategic objectives. On the skeleton plane, we further refine that structure, identifying specific aspects of interface, navigation, and information design that will make the intangible structure concrete.

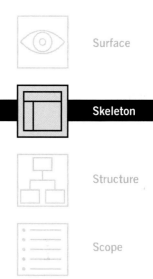

Surface

Skeleton

Structure

Scope

Strategy

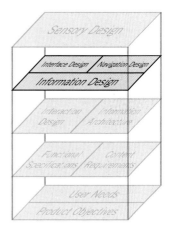

Defining the Skeleton

The structure plane covered in the preceding chapter defines how our product will work; the skeleton plane defines what form that functionality will take. In addition to addressing more concrete issues of presentation, the skeleton plane deals with matters that involve a more refined level of detail. On the structure plane, we looked at the large-scale issues of architecture and interaction; on the skeleton plane, our concerns exist almost exclusively at the smaller scale of individual components and their relationships.

On the functionality side, we define the skeleton through **interface design**—the familiar realm of buttons, fields, and other interface components. But information products have a unique set of problems all their own. **Navigation design** is the specialized form of interface design tailored to presenting information spaces. Finally, crossing both sides, we have **information design**, the presentation of information for effective communication.

product as functionality | product as information

skeleton

Interface Design / Navigation Design

Information Design

surface

structure

These three elements are closely bound together—more so than any of the other elements covered in this book. It's not uncommon to be faced with navigation design problems that begin to blur into information design problems, or to encounter questions about information design that turn out to be matters of interface design.

Even though the lines sometimes get blurry, identifying these as separate areas of concern helps us better assess whether we've settled on a suitable solution. Good navigation design can't correct bad information design. If we can't tell the difference between the types of problems, we can't tell if we've really solved them.

If it involves providing users with the ability to do things, it's interface design. The interface is the means by which users actually come into contact with the functionality defined in the specifications and structured in the interaction design.

If it involves providing users with the ability to go places, it's navigation design. The information architecture applied a structure to the content requirements we developed; the navigation design is the lens through which the user can see that structure, and is the means by which the user can move through it.

If it involves communicating ideas to the user, it's information design. This is the broadest of the three elements on this plane, potentially incorporating or drawing upon aspects of almost everything we've seen so far on both the functionality side and the information side. Information design crosses the boundary between task-oriented functionality and information-oriented systems because neither interface design nor navigation design can be fully successful without good information design to support them.

Convention and Metaphor

Habit and reflex are the foundation for much of our interaction with the world—indeed, if we weren't able to reduce so much of what we do to reflex, we'd accomplish a whole lot less every day. Can you imagine if driving a car never got any easier than it was the first time you tried it? Your ability to drive, cook a meal, or use a mobile phone—without being thoroughly exhausted by the tremendous concentration needed for the task—depends on the accumulation of lots of tiny reflexes.

Convention allows us to apply those reflexes in different circumstances. I used to have a car that invariably caused trouble whenever any of my friends drove it. When they started the car, the first thing they did was wash the windshield. This wasn't because they thought the windshield was dirty (though it probably was); rather, it was because they were trying to turn on the headlights. The controls on my car were different from the conventions they were used to.

Telephones are another good example of the importance of convention. From time to time, manufacturers have experimented with deviations from the standard three-by-four layout for the buttons on a telephone, such as two rows of six buttons each, or three rows of four. Circular arrangements still pop up from time to time, but these are becoming ever more rare as the rotary-dial phones on which they are based fade into the mists of technological oblivion.

It seems like the layout shouldn't make that much of a difference, but it does. If you measured the time a user spends trying to figure out which button to push on a nonstandard telephone, it might turn out to be something like three seconds per call. Not that big a difference—but to the user, those three seconds aren't just lost time. Those three seconds are filled with pure frustration, as a reflexive task becomes agonizingly slow simply because the rug of convention has been pulled out from under the user's feet.

In fact, the telephone's three-by-four matrix of digits is so well ingrained that it has become the standard for other devices that have nothing to do with telephones, such as microwave ovens or remote controls. Interestingly, the phone pad is not the only standard in this area: The "10-key" standard used by old adding machines, which inverts the order of the digits on the telephone keypad, is used on calculators, keyboards, ATMs, cash registers, and in specialized data-entry applications such as inventory systems. Because both standards use a three-by-four matrix, people can adapt to either with relative ease, though a single standard would really be the best solution of all.

This is not to say that the answer to every interface problem is slavish adherence to convention. Instead, you should simply be cautious about deviating from convention and only do so when a different approach offers clear benefits. Creating a successful user experience requires having explicitly defined reasons for every choice you make.

Making your interface consistent with others that your users are already familiar with is important, but even more important is making your interface consistent with itself. The conceptual models for the features of your product can help you ensure internal consistency. If you have two features with the same conceptual model, they are likely to have similar interface requirements. Using the same conventions in both places allows a user who is familiar with one to adapt quickly to the other.

Even where the conceptual models for features differ, ideas that apply across a variety of conceptual models should be treated similarly (if not identically) wherever they appear. Concepts like "start," "finish," "go back," or "save" can be found in a wide range of contexts. Giving these a consistent treatment throughout lets users apply what they already know from having used other parts of the system, getting them to their goals faster and with fewer mistakes.

Just as you shouldn't take the conceptual models underlying your interaction design too literally, you should resist the impulse to construct your product around a series of concrete **metaphors**. Metaphors for the features of your product are cute and fun, but they almost never work as well as it seems they should. In fact, they often don't work at all.

In some cases, you might be inclined to pattern the interface design for a particular function after the interface of a real-world object. Remember Slate's navigation in which you could "turn" the pages just like in a real magazine? Most interfaces and navigational devices in the real world are the product of the constraints of the real world: physics, the properties of materials, and so on. Screen-based products such as Web sites and other software have few of the same constraints.

Drawing analogies between features of your site and experiences people have in the real world might seem like a good way to help people get a handle on what those features are all about. However, this kind of approach usually obscures the nature of the feature instead of revealing it. Even though the association between the feature and its metaphorical representation is clear to you, it's just one of any number of associations your users might apply—especially if those users come from a different cultural background than you do. What does that little picture of a telephone mean? Will it allow me to make a phone call? Check my voice mail? Pay my phone bill?

Of course, the content of your site should provide some degree of context to help users make better guesses about what features your metaphors are intended to represent. But the more diverse the range of content and functionality you offer, the less reliable these guesses become—and at any rate, some part of your audience is always going to guess incorrectly. It would be better (and simpler) to eliminate that guesswork altogether.

Using metaphors effectively is really just about reducing the mental effort required for users to get around and use the functionality of your product. Having an icon of a phone book to represent an actual directory of telephone numbers might be just fine; having a picture of a coffee shop to represent your chat area is a bit more problematic.

Interface Design

Interface design is all about selecting the right interface elements for the task the user is trying to accomplish and arranging them on the screen in a way that will be readily understood and easily used. Tasks will often stretch across several screens, each containing a different set of interface elements for the user to contend with. Which functions end up on which screens is a matter of interaction design down in the structure plane; how those functions are realized on the screen is the realm of interface design.

Successful interfaces are those in which users immediately notice the important stuff. Unimportant stuff, on the other hand, doesn't get noticed—sometimes because it's not there at all. One of the biggest challenges of designing interfaces for complex systems is figuring out which aspects the users don't need to deal with and reducing their visibility (or leaving them out altogether).

For people with a background in programming, this way of thinking can require some adjustment. It's often very different from what they are used to. Good programmers always take into account the most unlikely scenarios (called "edge cases" in programming jargon). After all, the ultimate accomplishment for programmers is creating software that never breaks; but programming that doesn't account for edge cases is likely to do exactly that under those extreme circumstances. So programmers are trained to treat every case equally, whether it represents one user or one thousand.

This approach doesn't work for interface design. An interface that gives a small number of extreme cases the same weight as the needs of the vast majority of users ends up ill-equipped to make either audience happy. A well-designed interface recognizes the courses of action users are most likely to take and makes those interface elements easiest to access and use.

This doesn't mean that the solution to every interface problem is to make the button users are most likely to push the biggest one. Interface designs can employ a variety of tricks to ease users along the way to their goals. One simple trick is to think carefully about the default options selected when the interface is first presented to the user. If your understanding of your users' tasks and goals leads you to think most of them would prefer detailed search results over brief ones, leaving the Show Me More Detail checkbox checked by default means more people will automatically be happy with what they get, regardless of whether they took the time to read the label on the checkbox and make a decision for themselves. Even better is a system that automatically remembers the options a user selected the last time they stopped by, but this sometimes requires more technical acrobatics than would appear necessary on the surface, and as a result is impractical for some development teams to implement successfully.

Technology tools and frameworks have inherent technical constraints that limit the interface options available to us. This is actually both bad and good. It's bad because it limits our opportunities for innovation—some interface approaches that might be possible using certain technologies might be impossible to realize with others. But this situation is also good, because users who learn how to work with a fairly small set of standard controls can apply that knowledge across a wide range of products.

Interface conventions seem like they shouldn't change, but they do, if very slowly. New technologies sometimes bring the need to re-examine existing conventions or come up with some new ones. User experience designers continue to seek out new conventions for technologies like gestural controls and touchscreen devices. Most of the standard controls we see across a wide range of screen-based products originated with desktop computer operating systems like Mac OS or Windows. These operating systems offer a handful of standard interface elements:

Checkboxes allow users to select options independently of one another.

☐ Checkboxes are independent
☑ So they can come in groups

☐ Or stand alone

Radio buttons allow users to select one option from among a set of mutually exclusive options.

◯ Radio buttons
◯ Come in groups
◯ And are used to make
◉ Mutually exclusive selections
◯ Burma–Shave

Text fields allow users to—wait for it—enter text.

Text input fields let you input text

Dropdown lists provide the same functionality as radio buttons, but they do so in a more compact space, allowing many more options to be presented efficiently.

List boxes provide the same functionality as checkboxes, but they do so in a more compact space (because list boxes scroll). As with dropdowns, this enables the list box to easily support a large number of options.

List boxes
Are like dropdowns
But they let
You make
Multiple selections
Like checkboxes do

Action buttons can do lots of different things. Typically, they tell the system to take all the other information the user has provided via other interface elements and do something—take action—with it.

Buttons perform actions

Some technologies provide this same set of basic elements, but don't force designers to stick to using them, allowing a greater degree of flexibility in how the interface can respond to the user. Consequently, these interfaces involve a lot more choices to be made during the design process, and they tend to be harder to get right.

Dropdown lists can hinder users by hiding important options from view (left). Radio buttons easily display all the available options (right), but they take more space in the interface.

Juggling all the different interface elements and choosing from among them inevitably involves trade-offs. True, that dropdown will save you some space on the screen relative to a set of radio buttons, but it will also hide the available choices from the user. Having people type in the categories they want to search might put less load on the database, but it puts more load on the user; if there are only six to choose from anyway, maybe some checkboxes would be better.

Navigation Design

Designing navigation for the Web seems like a simple business: Put links on every page that allow users to get around on the site. If you scratch the surface, however, the complexities of navigation design become apparent. The navigation design of any site must accomplish three simultaneous goals:

> ▶ First, it must provide users with a means for getting from one point to another on the site. Because it's usually impractical (and even when practical, it's generally not a good idea) to link to every page from every other page, navigation elements have to be selected to facilitate real user behavior—and by the way, that means those links have to actually work, too.

▶ Second, the navigation design must communicate the relationship between the elements it contains. It's not enough to merely provide a list of links. What do those links have to do with each other? Are some more important than others? What are the relevant differences between them? This communication is necessary for users to understand what choices are available to them.

▶ Third, the navigation design must communicate the relationship between its contents and the page the user is currently viewing. What does any of this stuff have to do with what I'm looking at right now? Communicating this helps users understand which of the available choices might best support the task or goal they are pursuing.

Even for products that aren't information-oriented—or aren't Web sites at all—these three considerations come into play. Unless all your functionality fits into a single interface, you'll need some navigation to help users find their way around. In a physical space, people can rely to some degree on an innate sense of direction to orient themselves. (Of course, some people just seem to be perpetually lost.) But the mechanisms in our brain that help us find our way around in the physical world ("Let's see, I think the entrance where I came in should be behind me and to the left") are utterly useless in helping us find our way around in an information space.

That's why it's of vital importance that every page of a Web site communicate clearly to users where they are on the site and where they can go. To what extent users orient themselves in information spaces is a matter of some debate: Some people strongly favor the notion that users make little maps in their heads when they visit Web sites, just as they do in hardware stores and libraries; others claim users rely almost entirely on the navigational and wayfinding cues in front of them, as if each step they took through the site faded from their memory shortly after they took it.

It's hard for us to know just how (or how much) people keep the structure of Web sites in their heads. Without that knowledge, the best approach is to assume that users carry no knowledge with them from page to page. (After all, if a public search engine such as Google indexes your site, any page could be an entry point to your site anyway.)

Most sites actually provide multiple **navigation systems**, each fulfilling a particular role in enabling the user to navigate the site successfully in a variety of circumstances. Several common types of navigation systems have sprung up in practice.

Global navigation.

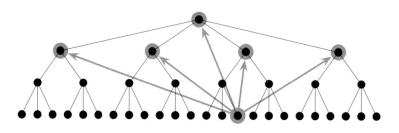

Global navigation provides access to the broad sweep of the entire site. The use of the term *global* here doesn't necessarily imply that this navigation appears on every page in the site—although that's not a bad idea. (We use the term *persistent* to refer to navigation elements that appear throughout a site; again, keep in mind that persistent elements are not necessarily global.) Instead, global navigation brings together the key set of access points that users might need to get from one end of the site to the other. Navigation bars linking to all the main sections of a site are a classic example of global navigation. Anywhere you might want to go, you can get there (eventually) with global navigation.

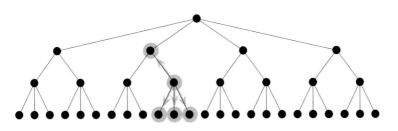

Local navigation.

Local navigation provides users with access to what's "nearby" in the architecture. In a strictly hierarchical architecture, local navigation might provide access to a page's parent, siblings, and children. If your architecture is constructed to reflect the ways users think about the site's content, local navigation will typically get more use than other navigation systems.

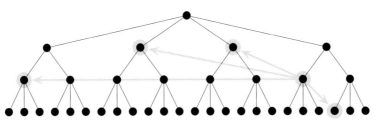

Supplementary navigation.

Supplementary navigation provides shortcuts to related content that might not be readily accessible through the global or local navigation. This type of navigation scheme offers some of the benefits of faceted classification discussed in Chapter 5 (allowing users to shift the focus of their exploration of the content without starting over at the beginning), while still permitting the site to maintain a primarily hierarchical architecture.

Contextual navigation.

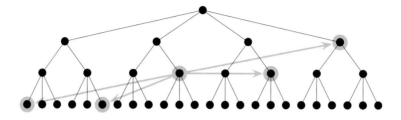

Contextual navigation (sometimes called inline navigation) is embedded in the content of the page itself. This type of navigation—for example, a hyperlink within the text of a page—is often underutilized or misutilized. When they are reading the text is often the moment users decide they need an additional piece of information. Instead of forcing your users to scan the page for the right navigation element—or worse, sending them scurrying to the search engine—why not put the relevant link right there?

Reaching all the way back to the strategy plane, the better you understand your users and their needs, the more effectively you can deploy contextual navigation. If it doesn't clearly support your users' tasks and goals—if your text is crammed full of so many hyperlinks that users can't pick out what's relevant to their needs— contextual navigation will (rightly) be seen as clutter.

Courtesy navigation provides access to items that users don't need on a regular basis, but that are commonly provided as a convenience. In the physical world, a retail store will usually post its hours of operation at its entrance. For most customers, most of the time, this information isn't all that helpful: Anybody can tell pretty quickly whether or not the shop is open for business. But knowing that the information is readily available helps them when they do need it. Links to contact information, feedback forms, and policy statements are commonly found in courtesy navigation.

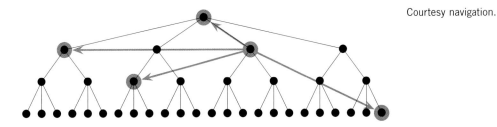

Courtesy navigation.

Some navigational devices aren't embedded within the structure of your pages, but stand on their own, independent of the content or functionality of your site. These are **remote navigation** tools that users turn to when they get frustrated with the other navigational systems you've provided, or when they've taken one look at your navigational systems and quickly come to the conclusion that they're better off not even attempting to figure them out.

A **site map** is a common remote navigation tool that gives users a concise, one-page snapshot of the overall site architecture. The site map is usually presented as a hierarchical outline of the site, providing links to all the top-level sections with links to major second-level sections indented beneath them. Site maps don't usually show more than two levels of hierarchy—beyond that is more detail than users typically need (and if it isn't, there's probably something wrong with your high-level architecture).

An **index** is an alphabetical list of topics with links to relevant pages, much like the index in the back of a book. This type of tool is most effective for sites that have a great deal of content covering a diverse range of subjects. In most other cases, a site map and a well-planned architecture should be sufficient. Indexes are sometimes developed for individual sections of a site, rather than attempting to cover the entire sweep of the site's content; this approach can be useful when you have sections intended to serve different audiences with divergent information needs.

Information Design

Information design can be difficult to put your finger on. But it often serves as the glue that holds the other components of the design together. In all cases, information design comes down to making decisions about how to present information so that people can use it or understand it more easily.

Sometimes information design is visual. Is a pie chart the best way to present that data, or would a bar chart work better for our users? Does the binoculars icon adequately convey the concept of searching the site, or would a magnifying glass be better understood?

Sometimes information design involves grouping or arranging pieces of information. We often take this aspect of design for granted because we are used to seeing common information grouped in certain ways. For example, look at this list of items:

- State
- Job title
- Telephone number
- Street address
- Name
- Zip code
- Organization
- City
- E-mail address

It seems a little confusing, because usually it looks like this:

- Name
- Job title
- Organization
- Street address
- City
- State
- Zip code
- Telephone number
- E-mail address

Even this arrangement could be clarified further:

- Personal information
  - Name
  - Job title
  - Organization
- Address information
  - Street address
  - City
  - State
  - Zip code
- Other contact information
  - Telephone number
  - E-mail address

This example seems pretty straightforward, but a slightly different list of items would prove more challenging:

- Power limit
- Rotor size
- Tank capacity
- Transmission type
- Median angular velocity
- Chassis style
- Maximum output

The key, of course, is to group and arrange the information elements in a way that reflects how your users think and supports their tasks and goals. The conceptual relationships between these elements really amount to micro-level information architecture; information design comes into play when we have to communicate that structure on the page.

Information design plays a role in interface design problems because the interface must not only gather information from the user, but communicate information to the user as well. Error messages are a classic information design problem in creating successful interfaces; providing instructional information is another one, if only because the biggest challenge is getting users to actually read the instructions. Any time the system has to give the users some information for them to use the interface successfully—whether it's because they made a mistake or because they're just getting started—that's an information design problem.

Wayfinding

One important function that information design and navigation design work together to perform is supporting **wayfinding**— helping people understand where they are and where they can go. The idea of wayfinding comes from the design of public spaces in the physical world. Parks, stores, roads, airports, and parking lots all benefit from the incorporation of wayfinding devices. Parking garages, for example, will sometimes use color-coding to give people cues to help them remember where they left their cars. In airports, signs, maps, and other indicators help people find their way around.

On Web sites, wayfinding typically involves both navigation design and information design. The navigation systems employed by a site not only have to provide access to the different areas of the site, they also have to communicate those choices clearly. Good wayfinding enables users to quickly get a mental picture of where they are, where they can go, and which choices will get them closer to their objectives.

The information design component of wayfinding involves page elements that don't perform a navigational function. For example, just like in parking garages, some Web sites have been very successful in using color-coding to indicate which section a user is looking at. (However, color-coding is almost never used by itself—instead, it reinforces another wayfinding system also in place.) Icons, labeling systems, and typography are other information design choices sometimes used to help reinforce a sense of "you are here" for users.

Wireframes

Page layout is where information design, interface design, and navigation design come together to form a unified, cohesive skeleton. The page layout must incorporate all the various navigation systems, each designed to convey a different view of the architecture; all the interface elements required by any functionality on the page; and the information design that supports both of these, as well as the information design of the page content itself.

It's a lot to balance all at once. That's why page layout is covered in detail in a document called a page schematic or **wireframe**. The wireframe is a bare-bones depiction (as the name suggests) of all the components of a page and how they fit together.

Wireframes capture all the skeleton decisions in a single document that serves as a reference for visual design work and site implementation. Wireframes can contain varying levels of detail—this one is pretty light.

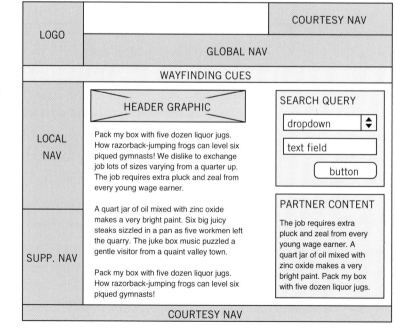

This simple line drawing is usually heavily annotated, referring the reader to architecture diagrams or other interaction design documentation, content requirements or functional specifications, or other types of detailed documentation as needed. For example, if a wireframe refers to specific existing content elements, it might provide pointers to where they can be found. In addition, the wireframe will often contain supplementary notes on intended behavior that might not be obvious from just looking at the wireframe and the architecture diagram.

In many ways, the architecture diagram we saw back in the structure plane is the grand vision for the project; here in the skeleton plane, the wireframe is the detailed document that shows just how that vision will be fulfilled. Wireframes will sometimes be supplemented by comprehensive navigational specifications, describing in more detail the precise composition of each of the various navigational components.

For smaller or less complex products, a single wireframe is sufficient to serve as a template for all the screens that will be built. For many projects, however, multiple wireframes are needed to convey the complexity of the intended result. You probably won't need a wireframe for each screen, however. Just as the architectural process allowed us to classify content elements into broad categories or types, a relatively small number of standard screens will emerge from wireframe development, based on the functional or navigational diversity of your product.

Wireframes are a necessary first step in the process of formally establishing the visual design for the site, but almost everyone involved in the development process will use them at some point.

People responsible for strategy, scope, and structure can refer to the wireframe to confirm that the final product will meet their expectations. People responsible for actually building the product can refer to the wireframe to answer questions about how the site should function.

The wireframe, being the place where information architecture and visual design come together, is often a subject of debate and dispute. User experience designers complain that visual designers who create wireframes obscure their architectures behind navigation systems that don't reflect the principles underlying the architectures. Visual designers complain that wireframes produced by user experience designers reduce their role to that of a paint-by-numbers artist, squandering the experience and expertise in visual communication they bring to information design problems.

When you have separate user experience designers and visual designers, the only way to produce successful wireframes is through collaboration. The process of having to work out the details of the wireframe together enables each side to see issues from the other's point of view, and it can help uncover problems early in the process (instead of later, when the product is being built and everyone is wondering why it isn't working as planned).

All of this makes wireframes sound like a whole lot of work. They don't have to be. Documentation is never an end in itself; it is only a means to an end. Creating documentation for its own sake is not merely a waste of time—it can be counterproductive and demoralizing. Producing the right level of documentation for your needs—and not fooling yourself that you can get by with less—turns documentation from a problem into an advantage.

Some of the most successful wireframes I've ever worked with have been nothing more than pencil sketches with sticky notes attached. For a small team in which the designer and the programmer sit right next to each other, that level of documentation is perfectly sufficient. But when programming is the responsibility of an entire team and not just one person—and that team is halfway around the world—something a bit more formal is probably called for.

The value of wireframes is the way they integrate all three elements of the structure plane: interface design, through the arrangement and selection of interface elements; navigation design, through the identification and definition of core navigational systems; and information design, through the placement and prioritization of informational components. By bringing all three together into a single document, the wireframe can define a skeleton that builds on the underlying conceptual structure while pointing the way forward toward the surface design.

chapter 7

The Surface Plane

Sensory Design

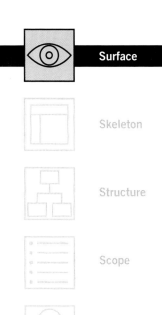

At the top of the five-plane model, we turn our atten-

tion to those aspects of the product our users will

notice first: the sensory design. Here, content, func-

tionality, and aesthetics come together to produce a

finished design that pleases the senses while fulfilling

all the goals of the other four planes.

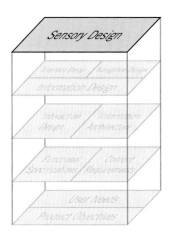

Defining the Surface

On the skeleton plane, we were dealing primarily with arrangement. Interface design concerns the arrangement of elements to enable interaction; navigation design, the arrangement of elements to enable movement through the product; and information design, the arrangement of elements to communicate information to the user.

Moving up to the surface plane, we are now dealing with the **sensory design** and presentation of the logical arrangements that make up the skeleton of the product. For example, through attention to information design, we determine how we should group and arrange the information elements of the page; through attention to visual design, we determine how that arrangement should be presented visually.

product as functionality | product as information

surface

Sensory Design

skeleton

Making Sense of the Senses

Every experience we have—not just with products and services, but with the world and with each other—fundamentally comes to us through our senses. In the design process, this is the last stop on the way to delivering an experience to our users: determining how everything about our design will manifest to people's senses. Which of the five senses (vision, hearing, touch, smell, and taste) we can employ depends on the type of product we are designing.

Smell and Taste

Except for food, fragrance, or scented products, smell and taste are rarely considerations for user experience designers. It's true that people sometimes develop strong associations with the smell of a product—such as "new car smell," which has proven so popular that it can be added as a fragrance long after the car has outstripped anyone's definition of "new"—but these smells are typically the result of the choice of materials in the product's construction, not the decisions of experience designers.

Touch

The touch experience of a physical product lies within the realm of industrial design. Industrial designers are concerned primarily with the user's physical engagement with a product. This entails elements of interface and interaction design (such as the arrangements of buttons on a mobile phone) but also includes purely sensory considerations, such as the shape of a device (rounded? square?), the textures used (smooth? rough?) and the materials employed (plastic? metal?). Thanks to vibrating devices, screen-based experiences can have touch dimensions as well. Mobile phones and video game controllers both use vibration to communicate with the user.

Hearing

Sound plays a role in the experience of many kinds of products. Think of all the different beeps and buzzes in a typical automobile and the messages they send: Your headlights are on. Your seat belt is unfastened. Your door is open, but you left your key in the ignition. Sound can be used not just to inform the user, but to imbue a product with a sense of personality. For example, any TiVo user can easily recall the variety of bings, boops, and bumps that accompany navigation through the TiVo experience.

Vision

This is the area where user experience designers have the most sophistication, because visual design plays a role in virtually every kind of product there is. For this reason, the rest of this chapter will focus on how visual design supports the user experience.

Initially, you might think visual design is a simple matter of aesthetics. Everybody has different taste, and everybody has a different idea of what constitutes a visually appealing design, so every argument over design decisions just comes down to personal preference, right? Well, everybody does have a different sense of aesthetics, but that doesn't mean design decisions have to be based on what looks cool to everyone involved.

Instead of evaluating visual design ideas solely in terms of what seems aesthetically pleasing, you should focus your attention on how well they work. How effectively does the design support the objectives defined by each of the lower planes? For example, does the look of the product make distinctions between sections of the architecture unclear or ambiguous, undermining the structure? Or does the visual design clarify the options available to users, reinforcing the structure?

Communicating a brand identity, for example, is a common strategic objective for a Web site. Brand identity comes across in many ways—in the language you use or in the interaction design of your site's functionality—but one of the main tools used to communicate brand identity is visual design. If the identity you want to convey is technical and authoritative, using comic-book fonts and bright pastel colors probably isn't the right choice. It's not just a matter of aesthetics, it's a matter of strategy.

Follow the Eye

One simple way to evaluate the visual design of a product is to ask: Where does the eye go first? What element of the design initially draws the users' attention? Are they drawn to something important to the product's strategic objectives? Or is the first object of their attention a distraction from their goals (or yours)?

Researchers sometimes use sophisticated **eyetracking** equipment to determine exactly what test subjects are looking at and how their eyes move around the screen. If you're just fine-tuning the visual design of a product, however, you can usually get away with simply asking people—even just asking yourself. This approach won't provide the most accurate results, and it will never capture all the nuances that eyetracking equipment can provide. But most of the time, simply asking questions is perfectly suitable. Another way to find the dominant design element is to squint at the page or blur your eyes until you can't make out the details—or walk to the other end of the room and look at it from there.

Then try to determine where the eye goes. If you're serving as your own test subject, try to notice the unconscious movements of your eyes around the page. Don't think too much about what you're looking at; just let your eyes take in the page naturally. If someone else is your test subject, ask them to call out the elements of the page in the order that their attention is drawn to them.

Generally, you'll find fairly consistent patterns in how people move their eyes—after all, these are largely unconscious, instinctive movements. If subjects report their eyes following a very different pattern from other people, they probably aren't really aware of their natural eye movements, or they're just telling you what they think you want to hear (or both).

If your design is successful, the pattern the user's eye follows will have two important qualities:

- ▶ First, it follows a smooth flow. When people comment that a design is "busy" or "cluttered," they're really reacting to the fact that the design doesn't lead them smoothly around the page. Instead, their eyes bounce back and forth among a variety of elements all clamoring for their attention.

▷ Second, it gives users a sort of guided tour of the possibilities available to them without overwhelming them with detail. As always, those possibilities should support the goals and tasks the user is trying to accomplish at this point in their interaction with the product. Perhaps more importantly, those possibilities shouldn't distract from information or functions that users will need to fulfill those goals.

The movement of the user's eyes around the page doesn't happen by accident. It's the result of a complex set of deeply ingrained instinctive responses to visual stimuli that all humans share. Fortunately for us as designers, these responses are not completely outside our control either—over the centuries, we've developed a variety of effective visual techniques for attracting and directing attention.

Contrast and Uniformity

In visual design, the primary tool we use to draw the user's attention is **contrast**. A design without contrast is seen as a gray, featureless mass, causing the user's eyes to drift around without settling on anything in particular. Contrast is vital to drawing the user's attention to essential aspects of the interface, contrast helps the user understand the relationships between the navigational elements on the page, and contrast is the primary means of communicating conceptual groups in information design.

When elements in a design are different, users pay attention. They can't help it. You can use this instinctive behavior to your advantage by making the pieces users really need to see stand out from the rest of the elements. Error messages in Web interfaces often suffer from blending in with the rest of the page; contrasting them by putting the text in a different color (like, say, red) or highlighting them with a bold graphic can make all the difference.

In a visually neutral layout (near right, top), nothing stands out. Contrast can be used to guide the user's eye around the page (far right, top) or draw their attention to a few key elements (near right, bottom). Overuse of contrast leads to a cluttered look (far right, bottom).

For this strategy to work, however, the difference has to be significant enough for the user to clearly tell that the design choice is intended to communicate something. When the design treatment of two elements is similar but not quite the same, users get confused. "Why are those different? Are they supposed to be the same? Maybe it was just a mistake. Or am I supposed to notice something here?" Instead, we want both to grab users' attention and to assure them that it is intentional.

Maintaining **uniformity** in your design is an important part of ensuring that your design communicates effectively without confusing or overwhelming your users. Uniformity comes into play in many different aspects of visual design.

Keeping the sizes of elements uniform can make it easier to recombine them into new designs as you need them. For example, if all the graphic buttons you use for navigation are the same height, they can be mixed and matched as needed without creating a cluttered layout or requiring that new graphics be produced.

Grid-based layout is one technique from print design that carries over effectively to the Web. This approach ensures uniformity of design through a master layout that is used as a template for creating layout variations. Not every layout will use every part of the grid—in fact, most layouts will probably use only a few—but every element's placement on the grid should be uniform and consistent.

Grid-based layout
ensures that diverse
designs have a shared
visual order.

However, because devices, screen sizes, and screen resolution can vary widely, applying grids to screen-based design isn't always as simple as it is in print design. It's easy to fall into the trap of adhering to a grid system—or any standard intended to ensure uniformity—even when it clearly isn't working anymore. The anarchy of working without design standards is bad, but the straitjacket of trying to work within design standards that are inadequate for your needs can be worse. Maybe the product has taken on new functionality that no one had imagined at the time when the grid was developed; maybe the grid just never worked all that well in the first place. Whatever the reason, it's important to be able to recognize when it's time to revisit the foundations of your visual design system.

Internal and External Consistency

Because of the way Web sites often have been produced—piecemeal, ad hoc, and isolated from other design work going on in the organization—they have been plagued with problems of consistency in visual design. These problems take two forms:

- ▶ There are problems of internal consistency, in which different parts of the product reflect different design approaches.
- ▶ Then there are problems of external consistency, in which the product doesn't reflect the same design approach used in other products from the same organization.

Good solutions to problems of internal consistency are rooted in an understanding of the skeleton of the site. The key is to identify recurring design elements that appear in different contexts throughout the various interface, navigation, and information design problems in the product. By isolating each design element from those different contexts before designing it, we can more clearly see the small-scale problem we're trying to solve, instead of getting distracted by the larger-scale problems imposed by context. Rather than designing the same element over and over again, we can design it once and use that design throughout the product.

For such an approach to work, we will have to check our work against the different contexts in which that element appears. Maybe a big, round, red STOP button will work fine for the checkout page, but it might not be as visually effective on the crowded product customization page. The best approach is to design each element, try it in various contexts, and then rework the design as needed.

Even though many of the design elements will be created in isolation from each other, they should still work together. A successful design is not merely a collection of small, well-designed objects; rather, the objects should form a system that operates as a cohesive, consistent whole.

Enforcing design consistency across media presents your audience—customers, prospects, shareholders, employees, or casual observers—with a uniform impression of your brand identity. This consistency of brand identity should be present at every level of the visual design of your product, from the navigation elements appearing across every screen to the humble button that appears only once.

Presenting a style on your Web site that's inconsistent with your style in other media doesn't just affect the audience's impression of that product; it affects their impression of your company as a whole. People respond positively to companies with clearly defined identities. Inconsistent visual styles undermine the clarity of your corporate image and leave the audience with the impression that this is a company that hasn't quite figured out who it is.

Color Palettes and Typography

Color can be one of the most effective ways to communicate a brand identity. Some brands are so closely associated with colors that it's difficult to think of the company without the color automatically coming to mind—consider Coca-Cola, UPS, or Kodak. These companies have employed specific colors (red, brown, yellow) consistently over the years to create a stronger sense of their identities in the public's mind.

That doesn't mean they use these colors to the exclusion of all others. The core brand colors are usually part of a broader **color palette** used in all of a company's materials. The colors in a company's standard palette are selected specifically for how well they work together, complementing each other without competing.

A color palette should incorporate colors that lend themselves to a wide range of uses. In most cases, brighter or bolder colors can be used for the foreground of your design—elements to which you want to draw attention. More muted colors are better used for background elements that don't need to jump off the page. Having a range of colors to choose from provides us with a toolkit for making effective design choices.

Just as contrast and uniformity are important to other areas of visual design, they play a vital role in the creation of color palettes as well. When used in the same context, colors that are very close to one another, but not quite the same, undermine the effectiveness of your color palette. This doesn't mean you only get one shade of red,

Orbitz has used a
limited color palette
(top) to differentiate
features and
functionality on the
Web site (bottom).

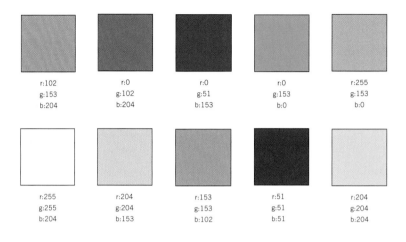

r:102
g:153
b:204

r:0
g:102
b:204

r:0
g:51
b:153

r:0
g:153
b:0

r:255
g:153
b:0

r:255
g:255
b:204

r:204
g:204
b:153

r:153
g:153
b:102

r:51
g:51
b:51

r:204
g:204
b:204

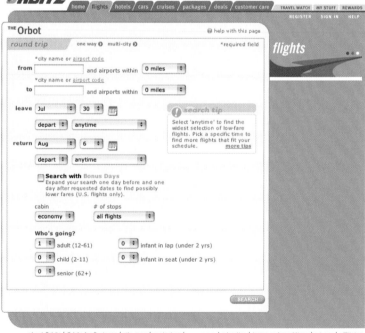

one shade of blue, and so forth. It means that if you want to use different shades of red, make sure they're different enough that users can tell them apart, and make sure you use each in consistent ways.

For some companies, **typography**—the use of fonts or typefaces to create a particular visual style—is so important to their brand identities that they have commissioned special typefaces to be produced specifically for their use. Organizations ranging from Apple to Volkswagen to the London Underground and even Martha Stewart have used custom typography to create a stronger sense of identity in their communications. Even if you choose not to take this extraordinary step, type can still serve as an effective part of communicating your identity through visual design.

For body text—any material that will be presented in larger blocks or that will be read by users in longer stretches—simpler is better. Our eyes quickly get tired trying to take in lots of text in a more ornate typeface. That's why simple fonts like Helvetica or Times are so widely used. They aren't your only choices, though; you don't have to sacrifice style to accommodate readability.

For larger text elements or short labels like those seen on navigational elements, typefaces with a little more personality are perfectly appropriate. But one of our objectives is not to overwhelm our users with visual clutter, and using an unnecessarily wide variety of fonts—or even using a small number of fonts in inconsistent ways—can contribute to that sense of clutter. In most cases, you won't need more than a handful of fonts to meet all your communication needs.

The principles of using type effectively are really the same as those for other aspects of visual design: Don't use styles that are very similar but not exactly the same. Use different styles only to indicate differences in the information you're trying to communicate. Provide enough contrast between styles that you can draw the user's attention as needed, but don't overload the design with a wide range of diverse styles.

Design Comps and Style Guides

The most direct analog to the wireframe for the realm of visual design is the visual mock-up or **design comp**. *Comp* is short for composite, because that's exactly what it is: a visualization of the finished product built up from the components that have been chosen. The comp shows how all the pieces work together to form a cohesive whole; or, if they don't, it shows where the breakdown is happening and demonstrates constraints that any solution will have to account for.

You should be able to see a simple one-to-one correlation between components of the wireframe and components of the design comp. The comp might not faithfully reproduce the layout of the wireframe—in fact, it probably won't. The wireframe doesn't account for visual design concerns, focusing instead on documenting the skeleton. Building the wireframe before we tackle the design comp allows us to look at skeleton issues in isolation first, then see how surface issues come into play. Nevertheless, the core ideas in the wireframe, particularly regarding information design issues, should be plainly evident in the design comps, even though they may not follow the precise arrangement presented in the wireframe.

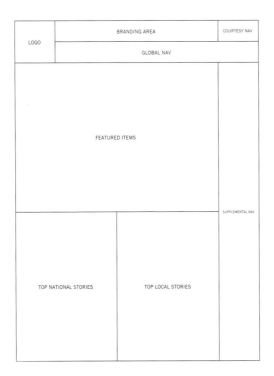

The visual design doesn't have to match the wireframe precisely—it only has to account for the relative importance and grouping of elements presented in the wireframe.

All of this documentation is, of course, a lot of work, but it happens for a good reason: Over time, the reasons for our decisions fade from memory. The ad-hoc decisions made to address a specific problem in a specific circumstance get all jumbled up with the decisions intended to form the foundation for future design work.

Another reason to document your design system is that people eventually quit their jobs. When they do, they walk away with a wealth of knowledge about how a product gets designed and built on a day-to-day basis. Without a style guide that remains up-to-date with the latest standards and practices, that knowledge is lost. Over time, as people change positions, the whole organization gradually suffers a sort of amnesia, as the ways things were done and the reasons for those decisions drift away to other parts of the company or back out into the workforce.

The definitive documentation of the design decisions we have made is the **style guide**. This compendium defines every aspect of the visual design, from the largest scale to the smallest. Global standards affecting every part of the product—such as design grids, color palettes, typography standards, or logo treatment guidelines— are usually the first things to go into a style guide.

The style guide will also include standards specific to a particular section or function of a product. In some cases, the standards documented in the style guide will go all the way down to the level of individual interface and navigation elements. The overall goal of the style guide is to provide enough detail to help people make smart decisions in the future—because most of the thinking has already been done for them.

Creating a style guide is also helpful in imposing design consistency across a decentralized organization. If your Web operations consist of a diverse range of independent projects being initiated and worked on by people in offices scattered all over the world, your site is likely to look like a random mishmash of styles and standards. Getting all those people to go along with a unified set of standards can be a lot of work, which is why responsibility for enforcing design style guides often resides higher up in the organization than you might expect. Having a style guide you can refer to is the single most effective way to get your product looking like a cohesive whole instead of just a jumble of tacked-on pieces.

chapter **8**

The Elements Applied

The elements of user experience remain consistent no matter how complex your product is. But putting the ideas behind the elements into practice can sometimes seem like a challenge all by itself. It's not just a question of time and resources—it's often a question of mindset.

Looking back over the five planes—strategy, scope, structure, skeleton, and surface—it all sounds like a whole lot of work. Surely such careful attention to all these details must take months of development time and a small army of highly trained specialists, right?

Not necessarily. Certainly, for some projects and some organizations, employing a team of dedicated specialists is the most effective way to parcel out responsibility for a product that's simply too complex to handle any other way. Also, because specialists can focus exclusively on a subset of the complete user experience, they often bring a deeper understanding of those issues to bear in their work.

Much of the time, however, small teams with limited resources can achieve similar results. Sometimes a group of just a few people can actually produce better results than a large team, because it is easier for them to stay in sync on a shared vision of the user experience.

Designing the user experience is really little more than a very large collection of very small problems to be solved. The difference between a successful approach and one doomed to failure really comes down to two basic ideas:

- ▷ **Understand what problem you're trying to solve.** So you've worked out that the big purple button on the home screen is a problem. Is it the bigness and the purpleness of the button that needs to change (surface)? Or is it that the button is in the wrong place on the page (skeleton) or that the function the button represents doesn't do what users expect (structure)?

- ▷ **Understand the consequences of your solution to the problem.** Remember that there's a potential ripple effect up and down through the elements from every decision you make. The navigation design that works so well in one part of your product might not quite meet the needs of another section of the architecture. The interaction design for the product selection wizard might well be an innovative approach, but will it meet the needs of your technophobic users?

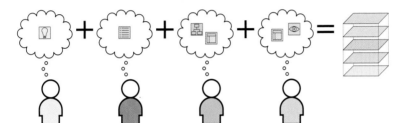

Only by having someone in your organization think about each of the five planes can you address all the considerations crucial to creating a successful user experience. How these responsibilities are distributed in your organization isn't as important as making sure all the elements of user experience are accounted for.

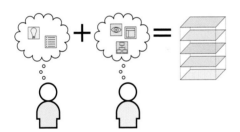

You'd be surprised at just how many of the tiny decisions that make up the user experience design process aren't made consciously at all. Most of the time, the choices made about the user experience fall into one of these scenarios:

- ▶ **Design by default.** This happens when the structure of the user experience follows the structure of the underlying technology or of your organization. Keeping the customer's order history and billing information in separate databases might work better for your existing technical system, but that doesn't mean keeping them separate in the user experience is also a good idea. Similarly, content that comes from different departments in the company might serve the user better if it is brought together, not kept separate.

- ▶ **Design by mimicry.** This happens when the user experience falls back on familiar conventions from other products, publications, or software applications, regardless of how appropriate those conventions might be to your users (or even to the Web itself).

- ▶ **Design by fiat.** This happens when personal preferences instead of user needs or product objectives drive user experience decisions. If orange dominates your color palette because one of the senior vice presidents is fond of it, or if all your navigational elements are dropdown menus because that's what your head engineer likes, you've lost sight of the strategic goals and user insights that should be driving the choices you make.

Asking the Right Questions

Facing the tangle of small problems to be solved in designing the user experience can sometimes be disheartening. Occasionally a solution to one problem will force you to rethink other problems you thought you had already solved. Many times, you will have to make compromises and evaluate trade-offs between different approaches. When you're in the middle of having to make these kinds of decisions, it's easy to become frustrated and question whether you're taking the right approach. The right approach is to ground each decision in your understanding of the underlying issues at play. The first question you should ask yourself (and the first question you should be able to answer) about any aspect of the user experience is: Why did you do it that way?

Having the right frame of mind about approaching the problems you are facing matters most. Every other aspect of the user experience design process can be adjusted to fit the time, money, and people at your disposal. No time to gather market research data on your audience? Maybe you can find ways to look at the information you already have, such as server logs or feedback messages, to get a sense of the needs of your users. Can't afford to rent a usability test lab? Recruit friends, family, or co-workers to participate in informal testing.

Resist the temptation to gloss over the fundamental user experience issues of the project in the name of saving time or money. On some projects, someone will thoughtfully tack on some form of user experience evaluation to the very end of the process—long after the time to actually address those issues has run out. Racing toward launch without looking back might have seemed like a good idea back when the launch date was set, but the result is likely to be a product that meets all the technical requirements for the project but doesn't work for your users. Even worse, by tacking user experience evaluation on at the end, you might end up launching a product that you know is broken but have no opportunity (or money left) to fix.

Some organizations favor this approach, calling it "user acceptance testing." The word *acceptance* is very telling here—the question is not whether they like the product or will use the product, but rather can they accept the product? This type of testing all too often happens at the very end of the process, by which time countless assumptions have shaped the user experience without ever being examined. Those assumptions can be extraordinarily difficult to uncover in user testing of the finished product, because they are hidden behind layers of interface and interaction.

Many people advocate for user testing as the primary means of ensuring a good user experience. This line of thinking seems to be that you should make something, put it in front of some people to see how they like it, and then fix whatever they complained about. But testing is never a substitute for a thoughtful, informed user experience design process.

Asking your users questions that focus on specific elements of the user experience can help you gather more relevant input. User tests constructed without an eye toward the elements of user experience can end up asking the wrong questions, which in turn can lead to the wrong answers. For example, when testing prototypes, knowing what problem you're setting out to investigate is crucial to presenting your test subjects with an experience that doesn't cloud the matter with unrelated issues. Is the problem with that navigation bar really just the color? Or is it the wording that your users are responding to?

You simply cannot depend on your users to articulate their needs. The challenge in creating any user experience is to understand the needs of the users better than they understand those needs themselves. Testing can help you understand the needs of your users, but it's just one of many tools that can help achieve the same end.

The Marathon and the Sprint

Just as you shouldn't leave any aspect of the user experience to chance, you shouldn't leave your own development process to chance either. Too many development teams operate in a state of permanent emergency. Each project is conceived as the response to some perceived crisis, and as a result, every project is behind schedule before it even begins.

Here's a metaphor for the user experience development process that I often use when describing problems to clients: A marathon is not a sprint. Know which kind of race you're in and run accordingly.

A sprint is a short race. Sprinters have to call upon vast reserves of energy at the instant the starting gun is fired—and they expend all of that energy in the space of a few minutes. Right off the starting line, the sprinter has to run as fast as he can and keep running as fast as he can until he reaches the finish line.

A marathon is a long race. Marathon runners need just as much energy as sprinters do, but they expend it very differently. Success in the marathon depends on how effectively the runners pace themselves. All other factors being equal, the runner who knows when to speed up and when to slow down is far more likely to win—or even to finish the race at all.

The sprint strategy—run as fast as you can from beginning to end—can appear to be the only sensible approach to a race. It seems like you ought to be able to run a marathon as if it were a series of sprints—but it doesn't work that way. Part of the reason it doesn't work that way is the simple physical limit of human endurance. There's another factor here, too: To accommodate that limit, marathon runners constantly monitor their performance, watch for what's working and what isn't working, and adjust their approach accordingly.

Product development is rarely a sprint. More often, there will be times when you push forward, building prototypes and generating ideas, followed by times when you pull back, testing what you've built, seeing how the pieces fit together, and refining the big picture for the project. Some tasks are best undertaken with an emphasis on speed; others require a more deliberate approach. Good marathon runners know which is which—so should you.

Thoughtful, deliberate design decisions will cost you time in the short term, but they will save you much more time in the long term. Designers and developers often lament the lack of attention to strategy, scope, and structure in the projects they work on. I have been involved in more than one project in which these activities were constantly under threat of being eliminated. Some people get

impatient with tasks that don't involve the production of an actual
site component like a graphic or a piece of code. These tasks are
often the first line items cut from a project that's behind schedule
or over budget.

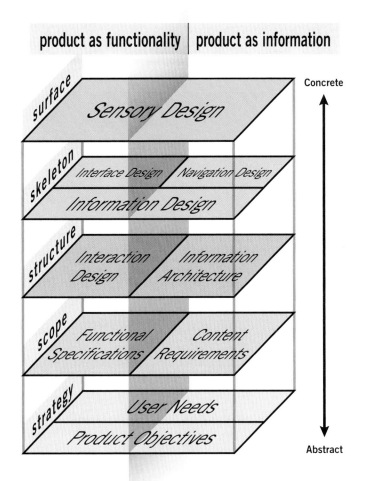

But these tasks were included in the project scope in the first place because they served as essential preparation for later deliverables to come. (That's why the five planes build from bottom to top, each serving as the foundation for those above it.) When these tasks are eliminated, the tasks and deliverables left in the project schedule feel uninformed by the larger context of the project and disconnected from one another.

When you get to the end, you've got a product that falls short of everyone's expectations. Not only have you failed to solve your original problem, you've actually created new problems for yourself because now the next big project on the horizon is to attempt to address the shortcomings of the last project. And so the cycle repeats.

Looking at a product from the outside—or coming into the development process for the first time—it's easy to focus on the more obvious elements near the top of the five-plane model at the expense of those closer to the bottom. The irony, however, is that the elements that are hardest to see—the strategy, scope, and structure of the product—play the most important role in the overall success or failure of the user experience.

In many cases, failures on upper planes can obscure successes on lower planes. Problems with visual design—layouts that seem cluttered or busy, or colors that are inconsistent or clashing—can turn users off so quickly that they never discover all the smart choices you made with navigation or interaction design. Poorly conceived navigation design approaches can make all your work to create a sound, flexible information architecture seem like a waste of time.

Similarly, making all the right decisions on the upper planes means nothing if those decisions are founded on bad choices made on the lower planes. The history of the Web is strewn with sites that failed because, although they were beautiful, they were utterly unusable. Focusing on visual design to the exclusion of the other elements of user experience drove more than one start-up into bankruptcy and led other companies to wonder why they were bothering with the Web at all.

It doesn't have to be that way. If you approach your product development process with the complete user experience in mind, you can come out of it with a product that's an asset, not a liability. By making everything the user experiences with your product the result of a conscious, explicit decision, you can ensure that the product works to fulfill both your strategic goals and the needs of your users.

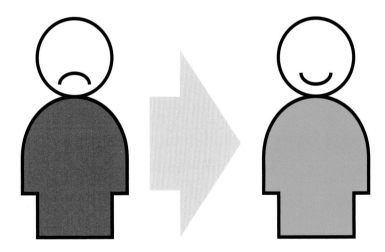

Index